Be a painter

make images by hand in the 21st century

Terrence A. Brooks

ISBN-13: 978-1461170297

The purpose of art is not the release of a momentary ejection of adrenaline but rather the gradual, lifelong construction of a state of wonder and serenity.

Glenn Gould, 1932 - 1982

We shape our tools. And then our tools shape us.

Marshall McLuhan, 1911 - 1980

You come to this book because making art gives you joy. Your art is evidence of your creativity and announces your singularity to the world. Joy is infectious and drives you to share your art with the world, but then you discover that the world - your mother being the exception - is indifferent to your art; and furthermore, views it through the lens of pecuniary instrumentality. *What can you sell that painting for? Why waste your time if you can't sell your paintings?* Most people feel belittled when their joy of creation is reduced to feeding a cash register.

In the 21st century we seldom encounter artisans who have spent years perfecting the simplest turns of craft. In our digital age, craft has been reduced to a button click. Convenience is seductive and we willingly substitute the monocular vision of a camera for the binocular vision of our eyes. But what price do we pay when we capitulate to a machine?

Children express vivid worlds in their drawings because their imaginations have not yet been contaminated by photography. The visual imagination of most adults, however, has been long conquered by photography. Listen to adults abandon painting with impatient frustration: *I can't draw*! Children don't say that. Adults are daunted because they assume the purpose of drawing is reproducing by hand what a camera sees, certainly a very difficult task. Since photography holds their visual imagination hostage, they can't discover other ways of drawing, which means they never cultivate their personal vision (i.e., what they see) or their personal aesthetic (i.e., how they see it).

When my son was four years old, he was fascinated by dinosaurs. I gave him pieces of paper and, while I worked at my desk, he sat on the floor and use color pens to draw his *emotional* vision of a dinosaur. His visual imagination wasn't yet ruled by photography so his visual knowledge of dinosaurs was derived from his plastic toy dinosaurs, picture books that his mother had read to him and occasional Saturday-morning television cartoons. His dinosaur was a sausage-shaped animal with four feet. He drew fins down its back and then fins along its stomach. He examined his drawing critically and then scratched out the belly fins. The head of his dinosaur was two parallel lines, like the sides of an open-top box that extended upwards and suggested ears or horns. The eyes of the dinosaur were two big circles with large dots situated on the sides of the box head. The mouth of the dinosaur - the most horrible part for a four year-old boy - was a long curved line that extended beyond the left and the right sides of the animal's head. That single line indicated a horrible, *scary*, mouth and expressed the *emotional* meaning of a dinosaur's mouth for a child...*the dinosaur could eat you with that mouth!*

My toddler son was capable of depicting the emotional reality of a dinosaur without being schooled in drawing, or perspective, or foreshortening and without the benefit of a camera. Today, my son is twenty-eight years old and has seen too many photographs; he would demur with embarrassment and tell you that he can't draw a dinosaur because he would endeavor to draw like an adult; that is, to reproduce the images of dinosaurs that he has seen in books, magazines, movie posters, etc. Gone is the dinosaur with a single-line mouth that extends right and left beyond the sides of a box-like head that seems topped with horns and has two large saucer eyes. That is the price we pay when we capitulate to machines.

In the 21st century we seldom witness a life spent perfecting an aesthetic and refining a vision. Such humility seems out of place in our world of instant gratification. Art absorbs a lifetime because it employs your eyes, your hands and your mind, living tools that change daily. Your eye grows more critical, your hand begins to tremble and your mind continues to invent. Tomorrow you awake to make art with these three organic elements subtly changed from yesterday. Little wonder the artist is constantly struggling to learn again, and to learn anew, how to make art. The path of least resistance is to let a machine make art for you. Visual editors suffer no shakes or devolution; click a button and the machine draws the identical line again and again. Letting a machine draw a line for you, however, deprives you of the struggle of drawing the line yourself, just as being whisked to your destination by mechanical transportation deprives you of the step-by-step experience of your journey.

You must continue to make art because the world needs your creativity. This book will help you understand the struggle to make art and your fears about being an artist. It will help you comprehend the reactions of people and the marketplace to your art and finally, this book will help you celebrate your art.

CONTENTS

This book is dedicated to GMB and ARB, artists both

Acknowledgements

I express gratitude to my family for their support, to Katherine Sotol, my first reader, and to the librarians, library staff and library resources of the University of Washington, Seattle. Thank you all.

Caught unawares by the 19th century

I was ten years old in 1956 when my family moved from Lafayette, Indiana to the prairie sixteen miles east of Edmonton, Alberta. A year later I moved to the 19th century.

An old photograph from Indiana shows me dressed like a cowboy sitting in a sofa chair drawing cartoons. In Alberta I learned how to play hockey in the winter and use a long string to snag gophers in the summer. I liked to draw, so my mother enrolled me in Saturday morning classes at the Shepy International School of Art, a series of rooms along a second-floor hallway in an old tenement building in downtown Edmonton. Professor Alexander Shepy, who had immigrated to Canada from the Baltic States after World War II, presided as the Master in the grand European tradition, dressed in a blue smock and black plastic bow tie. Here art was valued as a craft that demanded work and study: you might possess talent, money or some other advantage of birth, but you learned your craft from Shepy. No one parachuted into watercolor class for a week or two of amusement. Because drawing trains your eye, everyone began with chalks. Then you graduated to watercolors and, after passing a mastery test of watercolor technique, you moved to the adult room and to oils, charcoal and clay sculpture. I was living on the Canadian prairies in the 1950s, but Saturday morning I was in Paris about 1880 at the *Ecole des Beaux-Arts.*

Up a flight of stairs and a right turn down a hallway past several rooms where women looked up from their sewing, just where the hallway floor sagged, you began to notice the smell: generations of students had splashed the floor and walls with turpentine. The children's room was the first room on the right where beginners sat at small desks laboring with chalks and watercolors. To show his allegiance to Canada, Shepy had painted a portrait of Queen Elizabeth on the far wall. I did my first chalk drawing, a squirrel sitting on a tree branch, right under the nose of Queen Elizabeth II.

Along the hallway to the left was Shepy's office, a small fortress of European culture, art books and prints. During my five years as a student, I was in his office only twice. The first time I stared at the heroic Greek statue on the corner of his desk that had been knocked to the floor during an evening soiree and was now reconstructed with shatter lines and glue streaks. Shepy announced that I was ready to move up to the painting room. He gave me a wooden paint box with three brushes (two stiff hog hair brushes and a sable blending brush), his choice of oil paints (white was always *zinc white* and red was always *rose madder*) and an oval wooden palette. Carrying my paint box, I followed him into the painting room where he pointed to the second easel on the right-hand side, near the door. I was twelve years old and had arrived at last; I was about to become a painter.

The star of the class was an older teenager who wore a black leather jacket. He was busy doing a charcoal portrait of a gas station attendant (big angular jaw, smile, prominent cheek bones and a cap with a brim). I watched him create shade effects and then pierce the shade with a sharp black line, yet all I could see in his hand was a shapeless chunk of charcoal. Reaching clay sculpture meant that you had spent years mastering the various disciplines. There was a young woman who had matriculated that far and who breezed into our class about midday Saturday, saying hello to everyone and taking her sculpture out of a cupboard. Since our easels were nailed to the wall, the older students walked the row behind our backs, encouraging us but also pointing to messy patches in our paintings. Occasionally technical obstacles were negotiated: one day the sculpture lady lifted a canvas off an easel and judged the thickness of the paint by examining the canvas edge wise. I had never seen anyone do that and felt intimidated in this environment of highly charged craft expertise.

Near the end of our class Shepy circled the room and visited with each of us, critiquing our work. I stood up and he sat in my chair to silently examine my drawing. He would hold my pencil at arm's length to judge the lines and proportions of the model, and then mark my bad lines by putting two lines like these // over my wrong ones. Here is a description of how Jean-Leon Gerome (French academic painter, 1824 - 1904) interacted with his students:

> The reporter noted that Gerome visited the atelier to review the students' work regularly, twice a week, an exceptional diligence among the atelier professors. He examines the work of each student with the greatest care, but also with the greatest severity. He doesn't flatter. You don't await an encouraging word from him unless it is really merited. On the other hand, one can often hear, "that's bad, that's not it", as he walks past the academies [drawings after a nude model]. He never laughs. He smiles rarely, and his smile is more ironic than benevolent. You can't tell his favourites among the pupils, for he treats them all alike. This severity and this coldness do not hurt him at the Ecole, he is the master, the most loved and the most obeyed. (2)

Eager to graduate out of watercolors and move up to oil paint? Take a piece of watercolor paper and use a ruler to draw a tall rectangle three inches wide and nine inches tall. Prepare three pools of primary colors: red, yellow and blue. Begin laying pure red at the top of the rectangle, sweeping from side to side, but never going beyond the edge of the rectangle. Next, dilute the red and introduce yellow; this will create orange. Then introduce more yellow until at the middle of the tall rectangle there is a band of pure yellow. Now dilute the yellow and introduce blue; this will create green. Then finally, add more blue until at the very bottom of the rectangle there is a band of pure blue.

Go outside the rectangle, do it again.

If the band of pure yellow is not in the middle of the rectangle, do it again.

If there isn't enough orange, do it again.

If there isn't enough green, do it again.

At first I could hardly control the brush to keep the color within the sides of the rectangle. Even more difficult was the challenge of merging and balancing the color bands. Ruined attempts began to pile up. Draw more rectangles, but don't rush because a badly drawn rectangle negates everything. Mix more paint and get the intensity of the color just right. Now keep trying. A week later I got my first good one and then I mastered it; I could produce good ones with ease. Shepy looked over the half dozen perfect ones scattered on the table. I was ready to move on.

To our modern sensibilities, this watercolor skill test seems like a lurid punishment from a Dickens novel, especially if you happen to be a *digerati* who can engineer a three-color gradient with your favorite digital editor in about one minute: select the *rectangle* icon and then drag your mouse across the drawing surface to create a perfect rectangle any size you like, click to *fill* the rectangle and select *linear gradient* and then choose your colors. Move the little arrows along the color-picker slider to situate the color bands of red, blue and yellow. It's that easy.

But it also completely misses Shepy's point because he wasn't interested in three-color gradients. He was testing my mastery of mind, eye and hand over paper, brushes, color, line and stroke. His test recognized a very deep truth: painting demands the control and exploitation of *breakdowns*, in a Heideggerian *(6)* sense, that occur when the tool in your hand does something unexpected and demands your attention. The stroke-by-stroke psychological reality of painting is responding to an unremitting series of breakdowns. In Shepy's test, you swept your brush across the rectangle and immediately had to assess the width, the wetness and the color ... *breakdown!* ... because your next stroke had not only to adjust to the facts on the paper, but extend them in width, wetness and merging color ... *breakdown!* ... And with any stroke, at any moment, you might crash because you couldn't adjust to the multiple breakdowns occurring simultaneously. Genius painters respond well to breakdowns and even exploit them for novel effects; lesser painters are overwhelmed. Painting is all about handling breakdowns effectively.

This morning I was painting the portrait of a young lady and had defined her eyelid with a thin dark line. I placed in some lighter skin tone as the flesh of her eyelid and in doing so obscured the dark line ... *breakdown!* ... In re-painting the dark line of the lid, I used a tone that was purpler than my original dark line ... *breakdown!* ... I stood back and contemplated both eyes and judged the effect of the purple. I decided to keep it, but for balance had to add purple to the shadow where the eye inserts against the nose. The brush I was using was too big for this effect and narrowed the bridge of her nose ... *breakdown!* ... I widened the bridge of the nose with a light tone, but this reduced the contrast against the very light-colored tip of her nose ... *breakdown!* ... and so it goes, in a constant stream of breakdowns, judgments, reconsiderations, more breakdowns, further evaluations, etc. That one eye is purpler than the other will prove to some viewers that I'm an incompetent painter, while others will delight in my use of color. The color sense of most people is so undeveloped that they won't even notice.

By contrast, eliminating breakdowns is the goal of software engineering. Engineered products that break down are commonly regarded as failures, examples being boats that sink and airplanes that fall out of the sky. The conceptual structure of digital visual editors is expressed in computer algorithms, sets of instructions that the computer, the digital drawing program, the image editor, the photo editor, etc. all follow exactly. This conceptual structure is inherently deterministic; that is, computer algorithms can't produce any result not explicitly (or implicitly) in scope. No software engineer, especially one with ambitions of large product sales, would include the possibility of an *unintended breakdown* in scope because rogue software creates fear, and fear of software reduces sales of software.

Input parameters to a computer algorithm determine its behavior, thus the *line* tool draws lines, obediently - *mechanically* - following the steps of its algorithm. I can ask thirty students to choose the *line* tool and begin at certain XY coordinates and end at other XY coordinates. Thirty people will produce the identical line because thirty algorithms have received identical inputs. If everyone selects the same color yellow, thirty people will produce identical yellow lines. Everyone can then apply a *Gaussian blur* and the result is thirty identical, smudgy yellow lines. To introduce variety, each student could invoke some random numbers algorithm to generate an arbitrary *Gaussian blur*. Now we have thirty different-looking, smudgy yellow lines, but each one could be reverse engineered by deducing its random number and then applying the other input parameters. The products of algorithms are by nature predictable and, given identical inputs, reproducible. These yellow lines are *mechanical*.

After the class, I sit at my desk and select a sheet of paper and a yellow chalk. I begin drawing a yellow line and immediately notice that this particular piece of paper is slicker than I had anticipated ... *breakdown!* ... I adjust the pressure of my stroke, which means that I have now committed myself to producing a yellow line that exhibits at least two pressures ... *breakdown!* ... And then unexpectedly, this particular piece of chalk responds to its internal dynamics of cohesion and breaks into two pieces and I draw a sharp squiggle ... *breakdown!* ... I continue drawing, but with the newly exposed wider surface, which produces a thicker line ... *breakdown!* ... My ambition is to smudge the yellow line with my thumb, just as I did yesterday, but I notice that the skin on my thumb is rougher today than yesterday ... *breakdown!* ... And there is more oil on the surface of the skin of my thumb today ... *breakdown!* ... And in the early afternoon my hand shakes ... *breakdown!* ... And so on. The yellow line that I draw is a human artifact of that moment, those materials, me. It is *not* mechanical, not predictable and not reproducible. Tomorrow I could draw *another* yellow line, but I can't duplicate *this particular* yellow line.

Lifting my hand and studying the yellow line, I realize that the surprising squiggle suggests a figure that I had not anticipated a moment ago. The multiple breakdowns I experienced in drawing a single yellow line have thrown me into a maelstrom of unanticipated effects of line width, line pressure, line shape, line formation, all of which challenge my ability to handle breakdowns, provoke my creativity and, as I continue drawing, lift me off in pursuit of the novel, the unexpected, the creative.

Achieving unexpected, creative novelty with software is much more difficult because a machine can't escape its fundamental engineering paradigm. Manipulating a bit field is the purpose of a visual editor which excludes - *this would really extend its fundamental engineering paradigm* - the ability to prepare a piece of buttered toast. A coffee machine brews coffee, but can't manipulate a bit field, and so on. The tools we use to express our creativity have profound consequences: put combat boots on a ballerina and dance is affected.

Any machine that I place before my eye such as a telescope, microscope, periscope or camera, reduces both the amount and variety of visual stimuli in order to construct its special scoped view. A camera is a machine with a lens manufactured to industrial specifications that bends light and constructs images with digital image sensors that fragment light with alternating rows of red-green and green-blue filters. By contrast, the human eye is an organic device evolved to be sensitive to light and is not manufactured to any standards, nor submitted to any quality control check before being put into use. Human vision can be distorted by disease, trauma, and congenital conditions. One reason painters paint differently is that they see differently. One source of creativity in painting is breakdowns, and the source of breakdowns is the organic nature of painters themselves.

A bowl of blackberries in the lap of a two-year old child is a more powerful creative tool than any camera or digital editor. She will stick her hand in the blackberries and squeeze red juice between her fingers. She'll use the red juice to paint her high chair, her bib and then, in an unanticipated burst of creativity that smashes all paradigms ... *breakdown!* ... put a handprint on a wall. Twenty-five years later she'll use a visual editor that will restrict her creativity to manipulating a bit field and homogenize her creativity to the predictability of a mechanical Gaussian blur of a yellow line. If she continues to express her creativity through these tools, she constrains her creative potential to the limited range of their engineering paradigms. She could release her creative potential by pausing on the way home from work to purchase a yellow crayon and some blackberries.

Making something by hand is an opportunity to learn about yourself and the world. Pioneers, who homesteaded the prairies and found themselves in need of a chair, had to use their minds to conceptualize "chair-ness," their eyes to both critically and aesthetically judge their work in progress, and their hands to fashion wood into a new object. A faulty plan or a botched execution left them without a chair, forcing them to do it again and again, until they succeeded. Every successive effort was an invitation to experiment and learn. Buying a chair teaches me about my role as a consumer in a market economy. Making a chair from my own design teaches me about myself, what "chair-ness" means to me, about my tools, and about the nature of wood. The product of my labor gives me not only a place to sit, but a sense of empowerment. When I tell others what I've learned, I pass along craft wisdom just as

Shepy passed the craft wisdom of painting to me during the mid-20th century.

In the 1950s my father bought a Land Camera that used pack film; you snapped the photo and then pulled the film out of the camera and watched the image develop. I carried his camera with me about the frozen sloughs where cattails were banked with snow. I developed the film inside my shirt against the warmth of my body. Heat and cold affected the film developing process; I experimented and produced images of the prairies with arbitrary colors such as green snow.

My younger brother watched me set up my easel and pin my Polaroid to the wall. So began an appreciation of the difference between photography and vision - the Polaroids had their own color dynamics and were nothing like I had seen with my eyes. I sat at the end of my bed, looked at my brother who watched me with concern, and considered the aesthetic problems of copying it (the photograph) or recording it (the prairie slough) or perhaps painting the slough from memory by using the photograph as an *aide memoire*, or perhaps obsessively painting the image produced by the Polaroid, thereby making a painting that looked like a Polaroid photograph of a slough. I was fifteen and had a lot of dicey aesthetic problems to negotiate in the relationship between painting and photography.

The vast majority of Americans in the 1950s, however, didn't regard instant photography as just an excuse to make another painting. They were thrilled to capture an image so quickly and easily. In fact, these practical folks would have questioned the necessity of doing any painting since a portable instant camera could produce a picture of the slough in a minute. What is the point of struggling to learn to draw when a camera could do your work for you? If photography antiquated drawing, shouldn't the Shepy International School of Art have reframed itself as a provider of cultural amusement and encouraged dilettantes to parachute into watercolor class for two weeks of messing around? And after these new watercolor painters had satisfied their need for cultural amusement, they would have bundled up against the cold and passed a newspaper vendor along the snowy streets of Edmonton displaying Life Magazine that suggested that "the greatest living painter" was simply pouring paint out of a can onto a canvas on the floor. *(5)* There probably isn't a do-it-yourselfer in America who hasn't bungled the opening can of paint and splashed paint all over the garage floor. That's what Pollack appeared to be doing. The difference, however, was that his paint splashes were in Life Magazine and yours were in your garage.

Ease was the message received by the general public by such conceptual and methodological challenges to painting. It was *easy* to produce an image with a camera and it was *easy* to create art by pouring paint. In the 1950s you no longer had to work up a sweat to be a painter. Modern life had made painting by hand rare and obscure, an obsolete practice done with great difficulty by the old fashioned to produce a picture of a prairie slough that didn't even look "good;" that is, something that looked photographed.

1949 - Life Magazine publishes an article "Jackson Pollock: is he the greatest living painter in the United States?" *(5)* Photographed in action, Pollock drips and pours paint onto a canvas rolled out on his studio floor.

January 13, 1962 - The Saturday Evening Post publishes the cover painting "The connoisseur" by Norman Rockwell. This painting portrays an older gentleman standing in front of a large abstract expressionist painting, suggesting that the average American is bewildered by modern painting. This visual joke is presented in Rockwell's homey and near photographic style, which clashes ironically with the abstract expressionist painting portrayed.

1990 - Photoshop is introduced and suddenly digital images can be altered in limitless ways including transformations that mimic pencil, chalks or water colors and so on.

2006 - *The Photoshop Fine Art Effects Cookbook for Digital Photographers (3)* gives a step-by-step procedure for creating images in the style of the world's greatest artists. One formula provides a procedure for producing a digital image that simulates Van Gogh's sunflowers *(p. 130)*. I teach a class on web design and show a class of forty-one students how to do a digital Van Gogh.

2010 - deviantART (http://www.deviantart.com/), an online gallery with approximately 15 million members, introduces *Muro*, a HTML 5 tool for digital drawing. To promote *Muro*, a drawing contest is announced and deviants respond: "Just over 4 days later, deviants posted around 600 comments, with about 300 being contest entries." *(4)*

Each morning, as I eat my breakfast, I log on to my deviantART website (*http://terrybrooks.deviantart.com/*) to check for new comments and additional viewership of my images. I pay for a Premium membership, but am still exposed to advertisements informing me that I can buy a T-shirt displaying the deviantART logo. Points are available (80 points cost one dollar) that I can purchase and then give to other deviants as tokens of admiration. I can leave comments on their web pages. To lubricate the social aspects of deviantART, an emoticon called a llama (the South American camel-like animal) was introduced on April 1, 2010 and within two days 1,911,942 llama icons had been distributed by 414,940 deviants. *(7)* I count the number of llamas that I've received and feel inadequate if other deviants have received many more. (*Does that mean that they're better painters?*) An underground market in llamas develops where I can trade for llamas to adorn my site. Alternatively, I could join a covert group of mutual llama givers and in that way bulk up my llama total. This is addictive social media for artists and I'm hooked.

The social landscape of deviantART is balkanized into thousands of groups based on shared interests, iconography, technique, language, geography and so on. At the present moment I'm a member of more than twenty groups such as #FranceOfficiel, #Nature-Lovers, #All painters, #Traditional deviants, #Elite artists, #Illustrasyon [sic], and so on. If I wished, I could start my own group and so plunge into a competition for members in the struggle to become a high-status, prominent Super Group. Super Groups enjoy special website display advantages from the deviantART web servers, but tax their members to maintain their special status:

> ...*I direly need your help to maintain the Super Group status of our group. For the moment, it costs $59.95 or 4,796 points to be a Super Group for a year. And this is just for a limited time. After that, it will be $120 or 9,600 points.*

The psychological payoff of joining a group is the feeling of acceptance and achievement (*see! this proves that I'm an artist!*) when one of your images is accepted. The gate keepers who select images for the group might be founding group members, group administrators, or perhaps anyone with the spare time to wade through thousands of candidate submissions.

> *An Admin votes over submissions and comments the rejected ones providing a few words of useful critique. He also votes over join requests and sends Group Invitations to fellow illustrators who haven't already joined. The whole thing takes about 40 minutes a week, so we need people who visit DeviantArt at least once a week, have positive energy and who will be able to treat this like good fun rather than a boring duty.*

Occasionally a more old-fashioned issue such as "quality" arises. An administrator of one of my groups admonished us about the quality of our submissions and the need to "show effort." I e-mailed her inquiring what this means. (Her deviantART website described her as a 19-year old female from Toronto, but since deviantART exists in unverifiable cyberspace, "she" could be anyone from anywhere.)

> *I'm happy to answer your questions, just keep in mind, that I am by no means a professional artist, or anything of the sort. This is just my opinion and experience, being an art hobbyist, and admin to several active groups. ... [One group she administers] doesn't have any quality standards, so anyone can submit pretty much anything (except for a photograph) of an original character, and it will be accepted into the group. The only problem is that because of this, we get a TON of submissions every few hours. We accept pictures if they are submitted to the right folder, and sift through these submissions later to*

pick out anything that we feel should be moved elsewhere pretty much based on whether or not the picture is coloured, and whether or not it looks like it could have been done in 2 minutes by a 5 year old. Even if an artist is just starting out, and they haven't a clue about anything (anatomy, medium use, etc) but they still submit a picture that is fully coloured, even if it might be by grinding a pencil crayon into paper, then that means they're showing effort...

With digital art, it's a bit harder, because it's easy for someone to submit a messy sketch that they added a pattern or something to, for a background or some visual interest, so with digital art, it can be more about aesthetics. If a picture looks pretty, even if it is just a sketch or line art, we can assume that the artist put in some effort...

I assume that the majority of the members don`t look through every single drawing, or possibly don`t have the group `watched` at all. There are just too many pictures to go though. As an admin, I manually accept or deny each and every picture, and all I have time to do (while juggling a full time job) is glance at the thumbnail.

I uploaded the painting *La ville d'Ornans* (*http:// terrybrooksart.com/paintings/ornan/villeOrnan.htm*) to my deviantART website four days ago and it has been viewed 83 times and downloaded three times. Given that it is possible to screen grab any image presented by your web browser, it is impossible to know how many copies - versions - alterations - expropriations of this image currently exist in the unknowable recesses of cyberspace. By posting this image online, I have in effect given it away. To date, nobody has bothered to buy a print of the image.

The virtual world of deviantART blurs with reality as deviants voyage from real space to cyberspace, back and forth, as if paint on canvas and arty electrons inhabit one seamless universe. Most digital devices - your web browser and my web browser - have not been color coordinated. This means that the color you see is an artifact of your particular digital device.

> *When you work with the colors in a graphic, you are actually adjusting numerical values in the file. It's easy to think of a number as a color, but these numerical values are not absolute colors in themselves-they only have a color meaning within the color space of the device that is producing the color. (1)*

A deviant comments my painting of *La ville d'Ornans* "Love this! But I think you could do more contrast between houses and snow."

The look of the real object: The painting hangs on the wall of my living room and its appearance is a factor of the time of day and the light in the room. Turn on a light in the room and the painting changes appearance ever so slightly. At high noon on a summer's day it looks bright and at dusk on a dark winter's day it looks somber.

The look produced by numbers in a digital file: I photographed the painting (color shift one?) and uploaded the digital image to Photoshop (color shift two?). I cropped the image and then adjusted it with the Brightness and Contrast tool (color shifts three and four?). I uploaded it to deviantART, which given the task of storing half a billion images must use a compression algorithm (color shift five?). My deviantART critic downloaded it to his web browser (color shift six?). How many times has the color been shifted by digital transformation? What possible meaning can his critique of the colors of the snow have? Does he have a strong light shining on his monitor screen (color shift?), is he color blind in some way (color shift?).

Have we plunged head long into a digital quicksand and lost the distinction between a painting and a bitmap, between an object and an image of an object? Does my critic think that the bitmap actually represents the real painting? Has the vortex of arty electrons of deviantART obscured the reality of the painting hanging on my living room wall?

*

I stand before my easel with brush in hand, but wonder if I should be constructing a bit map. I trade paintings with other painters, but wonder if I should be uploading and downloading bit maps. I surround myself with the art I love, but wonder if I should be filling a flash drive with bit-map files.

My own painting craft repertoire, based on Shepy's legacy, grows with my years of experience. Visit my studio and I could show you the wooden table I use to support a sheet of glass that I use as a palette. I lay my oil paints out in a counter-clockwise crescent with white and black to the lower right. Earth tones are next, then at least two yellows and usually five oranges and reds and then three blues. I mix all my other colors such as purples and greens. Suppose you wanted to do a portrait, I could show you how to set out oranges, ochers, yellows and reds and then a touch of cobalt blue. I use a palette knife with white to smear through the colors to produce a series of hues and tints for skin tones. That's 19th-century craft.

I compose images on parchment tracing paper using soft pencils. After many preliminary lines and erasures, a shadow film of carbon builds up on the parchment so that I can use an eraser to sculpt out light points. In this way my line drawing becomes three dimensional. That's 19th-century craft.

I can show you how to build a wooden frame with corner clamps and stretch raw canvas. One of the most magical moments of painting is soaking the raw canvas with gesso and water to shrink the canvas to a flat painting surface. I can coach you on the feel of the gesso surface to determine the exact surface you want to use, whether you intend to use a wet, watercolor-like treatment, or a more scrumbled treatment with thicker paint. That's 19th-century craft.

The first Thursday of every month there is a Seattle Art Walk in Pioneer Square. There are a few older painters who work in oils or acrylics, but we are vastly outnumbered by folks showing digital products. I meet a young art student who is attracted by some boat pictures I'm showing. He asks me about my drawing technique, and he tells me that he's always liked to draw, even as a boy. He reminds me of the old photograph of myself sitting in a sofa chair in Lafayette, dressed up like an Indian, and drawing cartoons. I tell him about my techniques for drawing and building an image, but then he tells me that, at his school, drawing class is held in the computer classroom. It turns out that he isn't learning how to use pencils, charcoal or chalks. He wants to show me his drawings and wants my opinion of his drawing skills. He takes his computer out of his backpack and turns it on.

Drawing your inner vision

> *The pursuit of meaning through drawing is a process of embodiment, an unspoken dialogue between the self and the state that is to emerge. It is impossible for this state to be known by another. Mike Quantrill (5)*

> *Deprived of opportunities to draw, people are denied access to a vital and liberating mode of thought. Julian Bell (1)*

Cherish the images that pop into your head, they are messages from your visual imagination, your deepest well of creativity. It has promiscuously dropped a seed and given you the hard work of birthing your next painting while it wanders on to savor other delights. Ignoring these images is denying your own creativity.

Your imagination inhabits a magical world, but your hand must struggle with the material reality of craft: paper surfaces that are too soft or too slick, pencil leads that cut too deeply or smudge too easily, a brush that once could skim the slick of a baby's cheek is now withered and will only do for cementing the impasto of brick walls. Your hand negotiates all these craft contingencies that occur at the moment of creation (*I reached for the red paint - I don't know why - but the paper was too smooth for that type of paint and I didn't expect to get that smear, but isn't it wonderful?*) Artistic self discovery, the engine of your life as a painter, occurs when you create a virtuous circle between your imagination and the physical world. There is no more holy act.

To draw is to leap into the unknown because drawing transforms the imagined into the real. Your drawing is unknown until you do it, but facing the unknown is exactly what attracts a master such as Lucian Freud:

> *I think half the point of painting a picture is that you don't know what will happen. Perhaps if painters did know how it was going to turn out they wouldn't bother actually to do it. (3, p. 81)*

Any sortie into the unknown is dangerous so it should be no surprise that fear is the natural state of the painter. This morning I sat at the kitchen table and sketched a winter scene based on a newspaper photograph. I struggled over the amount of detail to include. *Fear!* Too much would make the painting tight and mechanical and too little would make the painting undisciplined. I set up a small easel in the carport and prepared my latex paints. I laid in the sky wash first and immediately stepped back. *Fear!* In what direction did my reckless, impulsive painting of the sky push me? I had sliced into the unknown to create the sky and the inexorable logic of the image and the color drove me to paint the snowy foreground next. *Fear!* At this point I had made two rash thrusts into the unknown, and now I had to step back and examine the sky and foreground together. Where was my reckless, impulsive painting taking me? Stroke, reaction, *fear!* Stroke, reaction, *fear!*

Those burdened with self doubt, the seekers after the comforting applause of society, will lament: *I can't draw, I can see images in my head, but I can't draw!* Abandoning yourself to your drawing may reveal something embarrassing to yourself and to anyone looking over your shoulder. The despairing cry: *I can't draw* is really the defensive complaint: *Why can't I draw safely, predictably and in a socially acceptable, or even better, admired fashion?*

Fearful painters want to draw safely. If you're an adult reading this book, it's already too late for safety. You must hurry and draw whatever your imagination shows you in an attempt to regain your inspiration. Ask yourself why Pablo Picasso mused: "I used to draw like Raphael, but it has taken me a whole lifetime to learn to draw like a child." *(8)*

Fearful painters who want to draw predictably deny their creativity because drawing is not predictable. Forget all your previous drawings and draw your next impulse without remembering who you are.

Fearful painters who worry about social acceptance are wasting their time. If you genuflect to public opinion, then you close the door to self-knowledge. Why struggle to be a painter if you are unwilling to learn about yourself as a painter? If your ambition is social acceptance this is the wrong book for you. Close it right here and put it down. Goodbye!

Self acceptance is the emotional threshold of original drawing. Once you step through the doorway of self acceptance, you enter the domain of craft materials and skill mechanics where you may be frustrated at *not getting it right* or surprised at having *no idea that it would turn out this way*. The answer to the question *why can't I draw safely, predictably and in a socially acceptable or admired fashion* is that original drawing is, by definition "original," which means not safe, not predictable, or perhaps not even socially acceptable.

Why is it so difficult to pick up a pencil and immediately draw in a manner that compels your audience to hail you as Michelangelo come again? There are several reasons why drawing is both mechanically and conceptually difficult.

Drawings are done by unique people

The architecture of your physical being influences your drawing: muscles, nerves, tendons of the hand and so on, as well as the physics of vision in your eye. Human physicality is unique: fingerprints differ, DNA profiles differ, your hand and my hand differ, both of our hands differ from the hand of Botticelli and neither of our hands is a 35 mm camera. Making images by hand forces you to recognize your own physicality.

As I age, my hand shakes with involuntary tremors. This frightens me because I fear that I will lose my ability to draw, but then I realize that I will simply draw in a new and different manner. The anticipation of future artistic novelty is delightful. Imagine how lucky I am to have a progressively shaky hand that will create marvels of drawing that will surprise me. This is not a self-serving rationalization, because it reminds me of the art school exercise of blind drawing.

I did blind drawing in art classes at the Nova Scotia College of Art and Design, and my drawings looked like a disorganized tangles of lines. Blind drawing is done by looking just at the model and not at your sketch board; this disconnects the draftsman's critical vision and demonstrates the link between drawing and physicality. Without the critical feedback of vision, your drawing is unlikely to resemble anything in this world. I taped my drawing to my kitchen door and every time I walked past I saw interesting relationships that suggested new paintings. My landlady, who didn't engage drawings with her imagination, wasn't impressed. She wanted drawings to look like photographs.

You can buy a book that illustrates the secrets of drawing like a Disney cartoonist *(the first circle is Mickey's head and the second circle is Mickey's nose)*, but this is substituting somebody else's creativity for your creativity. Using a digital image editor to edit somebody else's images *(click here to download this image!)* is substituting their creativity for your creativity. The fundamental reason you can't draw like Botticelli is that you are not Botticelli. All you can do is copy Botticelli, an activity that makes you a Botticelli copier, not Botticelli. You are not Botticelli; I'm not Botticelli, only Botticelli is Botticelli. Pause for a moment and consider that each one of us is condemned to be an original. You have to do your own drawing. And it's only by doing your drawings that you will discover what your drawings are about.

In your hand is a craft tool

The more sophisticated your knowledge of craft materials, the easier it will be to approximate your vision. For example, if your vision requires a thin, wet black line, you will probably be frustrated using a bulky chunk of charcoal. With time and experience your craft knowledge becomes sophisticated enough to permit you to predict results. I stand before a striking landscape and convene a strategy session with myself about craft methods: The sky will be a single blue wash that I can do with a wide soft brush. The dark trees in silhouette, however, would look best done in a heavy impasto and this suggests using my palette knife. A palette knife will mean thick paint applied with vertical strokes, which in turn suggests a solid horizontal placed below the trees of contrasting color and so on.

Deepening your knowledge of craft materials, however, is usually interpreted to mean buying lots of art gear. The art marketplace promotes the idea that successful drawing is contingent on using some product they vend. I once attended a workshop illustrating how to paint with a 49 cent brush; the workshop leader came supplied with boxes of brushes to sell. Bob Ross, a popular television painting evangelist, has a website advertising "Alizarin Crimson (firm 5 oz) - for landscapes" and "Alizarin Crimson (soft 1.25oz) - for florals." *(7)* While it is true that some oil paint is manufactured to be dryer, and therefore firmer than others, a little medium will make it as soft as you like. I'll bet that Professor Shepy didn't know that Alizarin Crimson is available in two versions: "landscape" and "floral." Question: Would I use both tubes of Alizarin Crimson if my subject were a landscape of flowers? Second question: How about a flower that looked like a landscape? Final question: Is this the art marketplace vacuuming up the dollars of the naive? *Yes!*

If good drawing depended on accumulating a big pile of art gear, then the richest among us would be the finest draftsmen. When you get a chance, examine the drawings of the very rich and see if they are substantially better than your own. Craft bric-a-brac is just that, and reflects the merchant's need for profit. It's to the advantage of the art marketplace to confuse the beginner by confounding the pencil with what the pencil draws. Short-circuit the whole art supply marketplace by picking up a stick and drawing in the dirt. Beach sand is good too.

The hand draws what the mind sees

Everyone has a visual imagination, an assertion confirmed every time someone describes his vivid dream to you. Cultivating your visual imagination is your daily duty as artist and like any muscle becomes more powerful with use. The opposite is also true: if you ignore your visual imagination, it will shrivel.

Drawing your vision requires that your hand serve your mind. Your hand, however, has its own agenda as your physical agent, which is simply to push the pencil along. Suppose you're drawing an imaginary face and you grip your pencil and stand with your nose two inches from the canvas. You draw one eye of the imaginary face *and architectural logic, not imaginary vision* commands you to place the other eye over there some place on the other side of the nose. You stand back and critically examine your drawing and it doesn't look right. You return to the two-inch position and fiddle with it, but the redrawing still doesn't look right. A circle of frustration begins.

Here's a test to determine if your hand has escaped your visual imagination: Erase hours of painful pencil scratching and then stand back *and your drawing looks better!* This effect occurs because the human mind fills in the missing parts. Now put your hands in your pockets and don't move! Contemplate the gestalt effect and weave it into the total vision of the imaginary face. When you have created a revised vision of the desired image then step forward and pick up your pencil again.

I maintain a playful relationship with my visual imagination. Working on a painting tends to crowd out any new visual ideas, and as I finish a painting I'm visually exhausted. This might provoke angst - *painter's block!* - but I dismiss all this negativity by making a bet with myself and marking my calendar two days forward. The bet is that in two days my visual imagination will have given me at least one; perhaps several visual sparks for my next painting. Now I can relax and merely wait for the images to flash before me.

But you can also provoke your visual imagination directly. I put a large sheet of drafting paper up on my drawing board and then sit down in my artist's chair about twelve feet away. My drawing board is an old canvas stretcher that I've used for years and is scarred with pencil, charcoal and paint. It's also warped and curved, all of which makes it a rich playground for the imagination. I pour myself a glass of wine, put a Schubert sonata on my CD player and let my visual imagination conjure with the surface marks on my drawing board. I enter a state of imaginative viewing that incorporates the marks and shadows of the drawing surface into the image of my mind's eye. Suddenly a face, a nose, the turn of a lip appears. At that point, I put my wine down, pick up a pencil and walk to the blank page and place a line. The process begins anew.

Perhaps there are some painters, who receive whole images, complete in all details, from their imaginations, but my imagination gives me only details such as the tilt of a head, a certain smile, the way a hand is poised. These details can be very distinct and fill my imaginative eye. Once my imagination fixes such a detail, however, it works like a 3D editor that can enlarge or reduce images, tilt them left and right, up and down. Make your visual imagination stronger by doing this exercise: visualize something, say, a cow standing in a field next to a milk maid who is holding a pail, and then imaginatively walk around them and examine them from all 360 degrees. The more you provoke such an imaginative image, the more concrete it becomes, and as its specificity increases, the easier it will be to draw. After a week of playing with the image of the milk maid and the cow, I drew the cow within minutes. I was merely copying the strong image that my visual imagination had already prepared.

Occasionally my visual engine spins out of control and an image obsesses me. For example, several years ago I was doing floral landscapes when blue birds began to insert themselves into my paintings. Then more animals appeared. Suddenly I was beset by the image of three blind mice holding white canes and striding forward towards the picture frame. I could see them marching forward with their large foreshortened feet. This image returned to me day after day as I rode my bike to and from the university and I finally had to release this demon image by drawing the three mice. I went through the front door still dressed in my bike gear, went downstairs and got out a pad of drawing paper and knelt down on the floor and drew it - *exorcised it* - from my visual imagination.

Once I had the mice sketched, then the other elements such as the kitten in the tram, the pig smoking a cigar, the lioness nurse maid were easy natural extensions. I painted *The three blind mice go for a walk* (http://terrybrooksart.com/ paintings/threeBlindMice/threeBlindMice.htm) and my visual imagination was at last satisfied. Asking what this image means, or explaining it in words, is futile. My painting of the three blind mice has no antecedent and no subsequent, it was merely an image that popped into my head. At best it can be understood as a snapshot of the location in my visual universe at some time several years ago.

Drawing is complex
Drawing exists in the visual domain where human beings have highly evolved interpretative abilities. We are very clever at reading a face in poor lighting conditions and

distinguishing one person from another. You are introduced to identical twins, for example, and at first glance find it impossible to distinguish one from another. But within several days you never mistake them. Computer scientists encounter these innate visual abilities when they build face-recognition systems. Computer algorithms can assess dark and light values in an image bit map and thereby reduce a photograph of a face to a line drawing. This produces a likeness, just as your pencil outline produces a likeness, but empirical tests show that recognition rates jump when the outlines are enriched with hints of facial mass. *(2)*

Years ago our drawing instructor at the Art Institute of Vancouver told us to draw into the figure, and using a line to hint at enclosed mass was what he meant. Examine a Disney drawing very carefully and you'll see that it is much more than a mere outline drawing. The mass of a Disney figure is suggested not only by the thickness or thinness of the lines, but by subtle curves at the ends of the lines. Drawing is complex because you must develop not only simple boundary lines, but boundary lines that hint at the mass they enclose.

When you draw you simultaneously deal with issues of perspective, foreshortening and modeling. I cautiously inch forward through this visual mine field by using approximation; that is, placing many lines, evaluating them from across the room and then successively erasing the many and leaving the few "true" lines. Beginners often burden themselves with the unreasonable expectation that every line they place must be perfect, and when their lines are not perfect, they become frustrated.   Lucian Freud abandons lots of paintings:

> *[An unfinished painting] looks promising and I've taken*
> *it up again on occasion. But whenever I did, I realized*
> *why I'd not carried on in the first place - in the same way*

that a specialist might say of a child, that one's not going to grow up right. I could tell that it wouldn't develop into a finished picture. There's something wrong. I have lots of paintings in my studio that didn't work. I feel in a way having them around keeps me going. One painting may go wrong after four days, another after longer. (3, p. 104)

Draw with a pencil in one hand and an eraser in the other. Since my visual imagination gives me just a few vivid details such as the angle of a lip or curve of a nose, I draw what I see, and then retire to sit, examine and contemplate. In moments, my imagination makes another leap, working with gestalt inner vision to suggest a link from the existing pencil line to the next detail. Inch by inch you work to a complete, original drawing.

Of course, the art marketplace will be glad to sell you a mechanical device to finesse these difficulties. David Hockney suggests that some of the old masters used optic devices *(4)* and Norman Rockwell, famous for his life-like results, used an optical device called a balopticon to cast an image to trace. Rockwell was a little defensive about his reliance on an optical device *(6)*

The balopticon is an evil, inartistic, habit-forming, lazy and vicious machine! It also is a useful, time-saving, practical and helpful one. I use one often - and am thoroughly ashamed of it. I hide it whenever I hear people coming. (6, p. 117)

The real danger in using the balopticon is that you will develop a lazy tendency to follow the image exactly

instead of following the creative idea or image within
yourself. (6, p.118)

If you covet the near photographic qualities that
Rockwell achieved, you too can buy your own opaque image
projector to cast an image for you to trace. Someone left this
comment on a website that sells opaque projectors:

I've started drawing portraits and caricatures from
photographs, and though I don't have too many problems
with features and shading, for some reason, getting those
first head dimensions right is difficult. But if I use ...
projector and get that head and hairline shape, right, the
rest of the picture is easy. As I become a better artist, I
may not need it any longer---but I sure am glad I have it,
now!

Recognize this pathology: small ambition, little
struggle, marginal growth. This person expresses the ambition
to become a "better artist" but has prostituted his creativity to a
machine. Photo editors such as Photoshop have transformative
filters that can reduce a photograph to a pencil drawing, a
watercolor painting, and a charcoal sketch and so on. If your
ambition is just to produce a pencil portrait, the path of least
resistance is to

(a) photograph someone,
(b) upload the image into Photoshop, and
(c) apply the pencil drawing transformation.

This certainly solves the pencil portrait problem *(Why*
waste time learning to draw?) and furthermore, you can

39

produce at least a dozen *(I really captured a likeness, didn't I?)* pencil portraits an hour, maybe more.

So why is drawing difficult?

Drawing is done by frail human hands using poorly understood craft tools to express an ephemeral vision in a domain where we have very acute visual abilities. Reducing the difficulties of drawing like this merely situates it in the same category as other human activities that take a lifetime to master such as playing a musical instrument and dancing ballet. Is it necessary to point out that the inherent difficulty makes it worth doing?

The only possible role of the art teacher is that of midwife, helping the student to recognize inconsistencies or self-contradictions in a drawing that inhibit the expression of personal vision. My sister visited recently, looked at my paintings and asked me if I could teach her how to draw. I replied that the best I could do is coach her in perfecting her own style by making her aware of her own work. I gave the same advice to my neighbor, a retiree who took an art class at a community college and showed me his first completed portrait over the back fence. After complimenting him on his effort, I told him to do fifty more, and then assess what he had learned about himself and his art. The point of this advice is not to clutter his attic with fifty portraits, but instead to force him to examine his arc of growth as he proceeded from, say, the 39th to the 40th portrait. I hang recent paintings in places where I can study them while I brush my teeth or tie my shoe laces, and ask myself what my last painting taught me.

While the inspiration of your drawing may be private, the object that is produced is public. Unless you are a hermit, you live in a web of family and friends who view your work and place it in *their* socio-economic value system or *their* cultural frame. Egon Schiele was imprisoned for his drawings, sketching Muhammad is dangerous in certain places, breast feeding images upset some folks, and then there are the eternal hot subjects of nudity, erotica, violence, impolite bodily functions, cruelty to animals, demeaning portraits of state leaders, social political protest...the list of provocative subjects is endless.

When I was ten years old my parents supported my art education and admired my chalk drawings of little animals. Forty years later, when I was father of two, teaching at a university, had been married to the same woman for 23 years, living in the suburbs, *and painting nudes,* my father wrote me a letter that included this admonition:

> *If you are willing to spend the time, money painting pornography - You're a 50 year old man and I can't make you change - that is for you to do. But I can, as your father, suggest you find out if your paintings have any artistic and/or financial value. You are not in a financial position with two children to educate to waste money and time for your own gratification; art that you can't display and need to hide away in some dark corner...In summary, why oh why do you spend so much time and money on an activity that has no value except for your gratification; and certainly is not cost effective.*

When he died my father was displaying about two dozen of my paintings on his walls (not the nudes, however). What my father's letter reveals is that the rest of the world may not appreciate your devotion to artistic self-development, and will demand that you justify your time and effort in terms of the marketplace. Original drawing is not only hard to do, but may well create something beyond good taste and threatening to social decorum.

Subversives of a social order should not expect applause from that same social order. Take out another piece of paper and sharpen your pencil. Now tell yourself that you're engaged in doing a very difficult thing that will likely go unappreciated by the uncouth member of the general public looking over your shoulder.

Reading "Art & Fear"

I was Christmas shopping at the University bookstore when I stumbled upon *Art & fear: observations on the perils (and rewards) of artmaking (1)* by David Bayles and Ted Orland. The pairing of "art" and "fear" in the title was unusual; I would have expected "art" to be paired with "joy" or "creativity." "Fear" expressed something negative, so I immediately leafed through the book and discovered that the authors were two photographers fretting over their ability to create artistic photographs and lamenting that their photographs were not recognized as art.

The book discusses being an artist in 20th-century America where art is a commodity and sales are a measure of talent. That provoked painful memories. In a cafeteria at the University of British Columbia during the 1960s, I was introduced to another student painter who flat-footed me by immediately challenging me with the question "what have you sold?" I was so innocent that I didn't know that the point of painting was sales, and I didn't have any sales. Here was a book talking directly to those who hunger for artistic recognition, but who fear that their art may not be good enough. Oh boy! That described me. I bought a copy.

Bayles and Orland express their anxieties in these two typical statements:

Fears about making art fall into two categories: fears about yourself and fears about your reception by others. (1, p. 23)

At some point the need for acceptance collides with the need to do your own work. (1, p. 42)

Disposable cameras are now so cheap that they are given away in bulk at joyous occasions such as weddings and graduations so that everyone, regardless of photographic skill, can click away mindlessly. People are encouraged to upload their photographs to the web and share them, creating vast online photo galleries such as Google Images, Flickr, Photobucket and so on. As I write this the Yahoo Directory lists 82 online photo albums, and the word "flower" retrieves more than 26 million images on Google Images.

In economic theory, marginal cost is the price you pay for the next unit of something. The marginal cost of your next image from Google Images is zero; that is, the price you pay is $0.00. Any object that is free and abundantly available is neither respected nor cherished. This means that every image - I include both photographs and paintings here - is reduced to just another glance in a disgorging emanation of web page slide shows, image strips, image thumbnails, image previews, image galleries, image carousels and so on. Free JavaScript utility libraries such as jQuery *(6)* place all these image manipulation algorithms within the easy grasp of any web designer. The extraordinary visual clutter of our lives today is due, not only to an advertising culture that scores when it hijacks our eyes, but to its technical accomplices who create more and more powerful tools to amp up visual display. As a result we are blasted by more images before breakfast than a person in the Eleventh century saw in a lifetime. The average peasant in the

Eleventh century lived in a hut, worked all week in the fields and only saw an image or a statue in church on Sunday. Americans in the 21st century spend hours each day watching television and the rest of time they're online; we're soaking in imagery.

In his survey of modern art, Edward Lucie-Smith points to the important role of photography in our lives:

> *The still camera, and its derivatives in film and video, has become the primary image-makers of our time. Only a very small proportion of these images are in fact bearers of any sort of aesthetic intention. One can draw a comparison here between the camera image and the components which go to make up a language - any language. We know that language can be used to make literature. We also know that the vast bulk of what is actually written has no pretensions to being literature at all. (8, p. 13)*

This means that the artistic photographs of Bayles and Orland are lost in a vast ocean of digital imagery created mechanically, inadvertently, unintentionally. Only the cognoscenti can spy a photograph created with aesthetic intention, while the rest of us paddle about in the swirling eddies of digital effluvia.

Painting suffers a similar economy of oversupply. I live in Shoreline, a suburb of Seattle, and within walking distance of commercial outlets such as Fred Meyer (supermarket and dry goods), Sears (department store), Big Lots (discount retailer), Deseret and Value Village (thrift stores). Yesterday I examined the paintings for sale in Fred Meyer and found a landscape of lavender fields in what appeared to be the south of France ($39.95 framed with glass), a charming still life ($39.95 framed with glass) and a smaller painting of a flower in vase ($19.95 framed with glass). My informal field study in Shoreline suggests the tentative conclusion that merchants price paintings by area, not by artistic merit. That is, larger paintings that cover more wall space cost more than smaller paintings. I found a painting of sunflowers ($27.99 framed with glass) that evoked Van Gogh in a section labeled *Home decor wall art 20% off*.

About fifty yards away in a Deseret Industries store, I found a landscape with church ($10 framed with glass), a very large landscape with the artist's name "Barbara Smith" across the bottom ($8 framed with glass) and a lovely 19th-century flower painting ($5 framed with glass). If you need a painting and aren't too picky, you can cover your walls for very few dollars. My empirical investigation into the availability and cost of paintings in Shoreline can be reduced to just a few words: paintings are everywhere and cheap ones can be had for the cost of a double tall latte. There is an economic implication to my little study: if your ambition is to get rich by selling paintings around here, competing substitute goods cost about a cup of coffee.

The handiwork of obvious amateurs, recognizable because their paintings lacked both glass and frame, were available in quantity. That the original art work of a loved one ends up in a thrift store shouldn't surprise, because after the loved one moves on, the painterly detritus scattered about can be sold or otherwise put to better use. I did a series of drip paintings on plywood many years ago and, when I returned home from summer camp, found that my father had nailed my plywood paintings into our rebuilt basement staircase.

Here's a thought: rummage through the 26 million flower images on Google Images and find one you like. Print it off and put it in your opaque projector. Trace the image on a canvas and then paint it. Who said painting was difficult? Foregrounding it against our noisy visual culture is, however, much more difficult. In short, producing an image is easy these days, getting someone to notice it is difficult. And if nobody notices your art, then maybe you're not an artist. *Oh oh, that's scary.* Thus we arrive at the dark fear at the heart of this book.

Distilling Bayles and Orland's fear

How does one become hailed as an artist in a market economy? Sales are the common yardstick of success in a market economy, which means that their fear is really "I'm not an artist unless I have sales." Photographers are particularly susceptible to this fear because the camera is a democratizing instrument that permits a lucky amateur to snap an image equal in aesthetic quality as any sacred image produced by a sweaty photographer after the most intense struggle. The oversupply of images means that their fear can be restated as "artistic validation results from selling something that has a marginal cost of zero" (i.e., you can download images from the Web for free). In other words, it's like selling ice to Eskimos or shipping coal to Newcastle, etc. Who is going to pay for an image when we're drowning in them already?

Goldhaber's "attention economy" *(2)* describes the critically scarce resource in the Internet age as human attention. There are simply not enough eyeballs to admire each pretty picture. The multitude of pretty pictures jostles for attention from folks who are already overstimulated by their digital toys and saturated with images. Finally, the full dimensions of Bayles and Orland's fear come into focus: "An artist validates himself by selling something that is already free and in oversupply." No wonder Bayles and Orland are worried.

They never reduce their anxieties to this brutal distillation, but it's the station where their train of thought will arrive.

If you plan on becoming rich by painting, but your bank account is depressing to consider, you can join Bayles and Orland and focus on feelings of artistic inadequacy. They note that *art is made by ordinary people (1, p. 4),* which suggests that, notwithstanding the few geniuses among us, the majority of painters spend most of their time learning their craft. If a lifetime is spent learning craft, then *most of the time you do work that nobody cares much about (1, p. 5).* Click these two ideas together and you realize that most painters struggle most of the time and their paintings evidence the struggle. Works of genius are rare.

Struggling seems to be the fate of even the most exalted in the pantheon of painters. When I leaf through Hulsker's *(4) catalog raisonné* of Vincent Van Gogh, my eye tells me that Vincent hit about one in four. That is, he set up his easel in Arles on Monday and painted something where the composition was a little off, Tuesday's work was also unfortunately flawed and Wednesday's painting had a little something wrong. Then Thursday ... *bang!* ... a masterpiece. The paintings of the following Friday, Saturday and Sunday were variously flawed and somehow not right, but then on Monday ... *bang!* ... another masterpiece. What marks Van Gogh as an extraordinary genius is his masterpiece hit rate of 1/4. If you are one tenth of Van Gogh, then your masterpiece hit rate would be 1/40. Why not be humble enough to admit that you're one hundredth of Van Gogh and have a masterpiece hit rate of 1/400? Use a 49 cent brush and you might be 1/4000 of Van Gogh.

Coming to grips with your low hit rate will temper your impatience for painterly glory and bring into focus the calculus of the time required to develop your art and the relatively few number of hours left in your life. Suppose that you're a weekend painter and talented enough to hit at 1/40. At that rate, given 52 weeks in a year, you'll do about one painting per year that will create a clamor among your viewing public. A low-talent, Sunday afternoon dauber with a hit rate of 1/400 would produce something noteworthy every eight years or so. A 49 cent brush and a hit rate of 1/4000 mean slaving away 80 years before you create something magical. Effectively, that means slamming away with a 49 cent brush for your whole life and having your survivors pick through the remains to find the single work of genius.

Why do artists spin visions of wealth if the marginal cost of a painting is a cup of coffee? Why do artists persist? Bayles and Orland suggest that doing art is valuable because it tells you *so enormously much about yourself (1, p. 5)*, but has the consequence of *living with doubt and contradiction, doing something no one much cares whether you do (1, p. 2)*. Bayles and Orland thus set up the cost and benefits of art in terms of doing something that increases your self-knowledge, but which may not be applauded by other people.

What is the exact relationship between methods of self-knowledge and applause from strangers? An avenue to self-knowledge may expand my consciousness, make me feel good about myself, make me aware of my place in this large world and permit me to peek into my own private fantasy world - think of painting, but also writing a sonnet or practicing the piano. Bayles and Orland, however, urge me to restrict my avenues of self-knowledge to those that other folks will applaud. Cross purposes? Self-defeating restriction? Somebody else doesn't like sunflowers and therefore I shouldn't do a painting of sunflowers?

If I consider myself an artist only to the extent that I generate sales, then the opinions of others (i.e., these would be my potential customers) really do make a difference. You can't sell carpet without a fine eye for your customers. Van Gogh, on the other hand, continued to paint without much commercial success; that is, he didn't let last week's poor sales hold him back. Bayles and Orland, however, worry about their poor sales ... *fears about your reception by others (1, p. 23) ... the need for acceptance (1, p.42)*...which signals that they've internalized the values of the market economy. Lack of sales is what a salesman - *not the artist* - fears most.

When I flip through Van Gogh's *catalog raisonné* and surmise that he hit one in four, I'm acting as a member of his admiring public; I'm not reporting how Van Gogh felt about the relative value of each of his paintings. The psychological reality of the painter is not the long odds of doing good work, nor the struggle through a series of paintings that will culminate with a masterpiece, but the satisfying exhaustion of finishing one painting and the shivering anticipation of doing the next one. For the painter, each painting is exciting; acquiring self-knowledge is always exciting.

Then unexpectedly, your viewing public responds to one of your paintings. Recently I've been doing a series of boat paintings and my daughter asked if she could have one for her apartment - she liked the way the wooden pilings were reflected in the yellow water below. *Bang!* Every so often I do a painting that somebody likes. Don't ask me if my hit rate is 1/4, 1/40, 1/400 or even 1/4000 because I don't know. My daughter might generously give me a hit rate of 1/4, my neighbor who likes Pop Art might grudgingly give me a 1/400 and the lady down the street who wants something to match her sofa might give me 1/million. So it goes. How people react to my paintings is not something I can control.

On the first page of their book Bayles and Orland wonder *if it was easier in an earlier age to do art than today*

(1, p. 1). They are nostalgic for an earlier age when paintings were more than just wall decor and perhaps had tribal, state or religious meanings; that is, when you could be recognized as an painter without having your artistic identity depend on sales. Whether or not it was easier to do art in an earlier age would depend on the nature of the earlier age. If that earlier age was one of building pyramids and you were one of the unfortunates condemned to hauling rock all your life, then spending a relaxing afternoon painting would have been impossible. If that earlier age was homesteading Nebraska and surviving through the winter meant following a plow all day, then taking time for painting might mean starving during the winter. On the other hand, if you were clever enough to choose 19th-century France and you happened to be Ernest Meissonier, you would have been feted by the State as a genius. Ross King describes Meissonier's acclaim during the 1860s:

> *The Universal Exposition of 1867 witnessed his coronation as France's -- and indeed the world's -- greatest living artist. Praise for him was unanimous and almost boundlessly extravagant. Scarcely a day passed in the spring and summer of 1867 without one critic or another declaring Meissonier's unsurpassed greatness....The Awards Ceremony for the International Exhibition of Fine Arts, held on the first of July, took place before a crowd of 20,000 people in the Palais de Champs-Élysées, hung for the occasion with banners and bunting. The ceremony was presided over by emperor Napoleon, with numerous other dignitaries -- including the Viceroy of Egypt and the Prince of Wales -- in attendance. Having easily received more votes from the awards jury than any other painter, Meissonier was*

awarded the Grand Medal of Honor. His coronation as
the king of painters was complete. (5, p. 203-4)

Having a government fete you in the fashion of Ernest Meissonier might be difficult these days, and even if the government did recognize your artistic achievement, if might not mean much. Consider that the United States has a poet laureate, but not a painter laureate. Pause for a moment to see if you can name the poet laureate of the United States. If you can't name this person, you discovered somebody hailed by the state as an artist, but who lacks general renown.

Bayles and Orland lament the great number of artists who give up after graduating art school - *the real killer is the lack of any continuing support system afterwards (1, p. 12).* That is, if there no sales, people stop doing art. These must be the art students who paint in order to get rich. Believe it or not, some painters do become rich and famous. Flip through the double issue of Life Magazine, December 27, 1968 that crowned Pablo Picasso as the artistic genius of the 20th Century *(7)*. Recently Damien Hirst sold a diamond skull for about $100 million *(3)*. Living in a market economy doesn't stop you from doing art, it simply requires you to cast your art as a commodity which you may or may not want to do. Your choice. Deliberating about this choice will ultimately reveal why you paint in the first place.

I was displaying paintings at the Pioneer Square art walk and a homeless man came over to share his art with me. He opened his backpack and took out a folded piece of cardboard where he had written in pencil "Need food." Inside the folded cardboard were his drawings. Meeting such a person demonstrates that you can be homeless and still do art. Art as a consumer object is not about the artist, but about the purchaser, who may not share your tastes, and may be really trying to find something that matches the particular shade of an orange sofa.

How the public perceives you and your work is the public's business, a matter best left to the public. If you spend your time trying to manipulate public opinion, then you are actually more interested in public relations than painting. If this is the case, why paint in the first place? If your life goal is scamming a few quick dollars and getting your face in the papers, forget painting and go rob a bank.

Dollars for painting

Suppose you get a creative urge when you contemplate the big empty wall over your new sofa. You've always coveted a painting of a wind-blown seagull hovering over an enormous ocean wave that is about to crash on a sandy beach. Surely, painting a wave and a bird can't be too difficult. A wave is just a big blue smear topped with white foam and a seagull is just a V-shaped white thing in the middle of the sky. You decide to paint it yourself.

Economists use the concept of "opportunity cost" to express the cost of the next-best choice. In this case, based on my survey of available paintings in Shoreline, the next-best choice would cost less than ten dollars. Spend ten minutes and ten dollars in one of several stores nearby and you'll return home with a painting of a wave, or some boats, or some boats on a wave, or some waves with a seagull, etc. It might even be framed.

A commercial canvas stretcher, 36 x 48 inches, will cost about ninety dollars and three brushes (a big one for painting the expanse of the blue ocean, a smaller one for the bird and the curlicues of foam, and a tiny one for the details of the bird's beak, etc.) will cost about thirty dollars. Buying paint is more problematic because both color sense and snobbery is involved. "Student" quality paint costs about eight dollars per small tube, and I would suggest two blue colors (a cold dark blue and a lighter, brighter blue), a yellow (we can create green by mixing yellow and blue), some contrast colors for the beach such as orange and brown, and then finally a red (mixing red and blue will give us get a purple for the details of the bird). Of course, you'll need a large tube of white. Let's spend a minimum of sixty dollars on paint. Some medium to thin the oil will be another ten dollars. You can prop the canvas stretcher on a chair, use toilet paper to clean your brushes and an old dinner plate can serve as a palette.

With nearly two hundred dollars invested at this point, you're ready to be creative. Pour yourself a coffee, contemplate the dazzling whiteness of your canvas stretcher, kick-start the creative engine, squeeze out some blue paint and say hello to a big blue wave crashing on a beach.

Ten minutes later, as you stand back in critical regard, you realize that sea water is not one shade of blue, and blue water against blue sky means that most of your painting is blue. White foam is more than just dollops of white paint and getting a wind-blown seagull to look like a wind-blown seagull is harder to do than it sounds. You mix dark purple for the fine details of the seagull, but another critical look suggests that if someone were on a beach and a seagull flew past a thousand yards away, the bird's eye wouldn't appear as a dark purple disk the size of a half dollar.

Learning your craft is a life-long battle and your blue wave painting is merely the first skirmish. If I were your neighbor, and you proudly exhibited your new blue-wave painting over the back fence, I would suggest that you do forty nine more wave paintings and then return to tell me what you've learned about painting waves. Pondering my advice, you calculate that fifty canvas stretchers at ninety dollars each would be more than four thousand dollars, which prompts your wife to remind you that "our children need shoes." Just about then your wife gratuitously observes that "the seagull looks weird" and after hearing their Mother's comment, your kids begin to sing-song that the seagull looks weird. With that kind of chilly encouragement and the calculation that your ambition to become a painter will cost thousands of dollars, you go out to the garden at midnight, dig a big hole and say goodbye to your blue-wave painting.

Does this mean that only the rich can paint? "Do art everyday" was the sign over the doorway of the art school of the Montreal Museum of Fine Arts in 1970. While this sentiment is admirable, you won't paint everyday if it requires lugging things around and pulling things out of cupboards. On the other hand, you can do art everyday if it is integrated into your everyday living arrangements and the required art supplies don't bankrupt you. Nowadays, it isn't necessary to run away to Tahiti to become a painter. Do you spend more than two dollars per day on a fancy coffee? If doing a painting rivals the cost of a cup of fancy coffee, then you can do art every day.

A place for painting

My atelier, about twelve square feet, is one corner of our rumpus room. An old rug on the floor catches drips and I share a second-hand chair with the cat and dog. My palette is a sheet of glass on top of a home-made wooden table. I get extra illumination from a fluorescent light that I bought new and which is my most expensive piece of art equipment. The "artist's chair" is available and waiting for me; I can sit there anytime and contemplate my work. My wife shouts down the stairs and the kids wander past.

Build your own easel

Over the years I have owned several wooden easels and about 25 years ago I salvaged the metal parts from one of them and built a tripod easel about eight feet tall. I drilled holes every four inches in the two forward legs for wooden pegs. By moving the pegs I can shift my painting up and down at my convenience. My homemade easel sits across from the artist's chair and after 25 years, it's covered with paint. You could splash paint on solid oak, but splashing paint on fancy wood doesn't make you a fancy painter.

Everyone can dream, however, so pause for a moment to drool over the advertising copy of a $700 easel:

> *This solid oak easel accommodates canvases up to 8-feet high, and features double-laminated quad base and side frames for strength and stability. A variety of easy settings adjusts the angle and raise or lower the canvas for work in sitting or standing positions. An extension on the frame slides up to give large paintings extra stability, and a middle tray is included which supports smaller work. A handy utility tray has two stainless steel canisters to hold brushes or solvents.*

Paint good enough to throw away

Paint will be your greatest expense, and unbelievably, you'll throw most of your expensive paint away.

Inhale slowly and re-read the previous sentence.

If you spend a lifetime learning your craft, then most of your paint will be used for "student work" (canvasses that you'll throw away), a lot of paint will dry on your palette (you'll scrape it off and throw it away), or it will be caught in your brushes (you'll clean your brushes and throw more paint away). If you are fated to do just a few masterpieces in your lifetime, then a very small part of your paint will end up in a masterpiece. Most of it will be thrown away, one way or another.

The art marketplace sells paint by exploiting your insecurities about being an unknown painter, your fears of not having real talent and your yearnings for artistic glory. Their emotional wedge is that maybe, *just maybe*, if you mess around with expensive paint, your messes will be high quality messes. If there were a causal relationship between the money spent on art supplies and aesthetic achievement, a lot of rich folks would suddenly find themselves famous painters. That's not the reality I observe. Consider the rhetoric used to convince you that spending eighty dollars for a tube of paint will make you a better painter:

> *The next generation of oils, a collection of professional, extra-fine colors reinvents your palette and redefines quality. Utilizing the time-honored, exacting methods perfected for over one hundred years, these paints are as highly pigmented, smooth and luminous as ever. Still dense, yet buttery, an updated texture with firmer body accommodates the requirements of 21st century artists.*

You could do your blue-wave painting using *dense, yet buttery* paint that costs eighty dollars per tube, but a seagull that looks crappy in cheap paint will look just as crappy in expensive paint. Expensive paint won't shield you from the ridicule of your children, nor will it prevent a midnight garden interment.

I do my ambitious work in oils, but for amusement I have worked in acrylics and attempt lively scenes of boats at anchor. But I was shocked at the cost of acrylic paint the last time I emptied my wallet at my art supply store and I swore no more. For my boat paintings, I now use latex house paint, which is one sixth of the cost of acrylic paint, and available in any hardware store. House paint comes in a wide range of colors, but a few minutes before the color chip display reveals that few people desire a house colored a deep hue such Rose Madder or French Ultramarine Blue. I thicken the latex paint with corn starch, and the result can be troweled on with a palette knife, but also thins out for watercolor wash effects.

I follow my own advice: to learn how to paint boats with latex house paint, I started a series of fifty boat pictures. I'm using canvas boards, 12 x 16 inches, each of which cost me about $1.75 delivered to my front door. I use about five cents of house paint per painting. After I finish the series, if you buy me a fancy coffee, I will be able to tell you *exactly* how to paint boats with latex house paint. Each of these paintings cost me less than two dollars - less than a cup of fancy coffee - so I can do art everyday and still buy shoes for my children.

Build your own canvas stretchers

Very few starving artists are rich enough to spend ninety dollars on commercial canvas stretchers, the vast majority of which will be thrown away in the endless struggle of skill improvement. Stretching your own canvas and preparing your preferred painting surface is one of those distant 19th-century skills that is hard to find in the suburbs of America today, and if your town doesn't include a 19th-century artisan, then the art supply marketplace has you in its cross hairs. You either fork over your dollars for commercial stretchers, or forsake oil painting as a hobby for the rich. Survey these typical prices for canvas stretchers that would force the average starving artist to empty his wallet:

Size (inches)	Cost (dollars)
24 x 30	27.71
24 x 36	31.67
24 x 48	39.38
30 x 40	41.77
30 x 48	96.22
36 x 36	80.99
36 x 48	97.08
36 x 60	119.29
36 x 72	130.52
48 x 60	135.35

But it's not the shocking prices of these prepared canvasses that are the real problem. The most profound problem with using a commercial stretcher is lost of aesthetic control. The investment of big bucks for a commercial stretcher psychologically primes you to fit your image to the purchased size and shape, *which is exactly the wrong thing to do*. You should let your image grow to its natural size and shape, and then build a stretcher to fit it.

As I draw the image for a painting I'm often surprised by things that clamor to be included or the many anticipated good parts that I abandon. The center of gravity of your image may shift as it develops. More than once I've turned my drawing ninety degrees and made a wide image into a tall image. Finally, there's the framing strategy of placing your image inside a big space (and thereby making it appear small), stuffing your image into a small space (and thereby making it appear larger) or placing your image to the left or right of center and so on. Draw your image first and then place it on a canvas stretcher that is sized and shaped to reinforce the meaning of your painting. *Don't let your creativity be dictated by commercial stretcher dimensions.*

My serious work begins with croquis (i.e., sketches) and then several weeks of drawing a full-size cartoon of the intended painting on tracing paper. After my image is established, I outline it with vertical and horizontal lines on the cartoon, which indicates the dimensions and shape of the stretcher I need. I buy raw cotton canvas and wood sticks that are 1" x 2" and six feet long. I build my own stretcher on the floor of my atelier using corner clamps and then staple the raw cotton to the stretcher. I take it out to the driveway and slop it down with water and acrylic gesso (both my kids volunteer to help with this part of the process). One of the magic moments of being a painter is watching the raw cotton shrink to a marvelous drum-tight surface on the wooden chassis. I apply a second coat of gesso to strengthen the face of the stretcher, and then prepare my preferred painting surface: a gray green shade of latex paint that emulates the neutral background used by French academic painter William-Adolphe Bouguereau (1825-1905). My perfectly sized, and historically accurate, canvas stretcher costs between eleven and twelve dollars:

Two 1" x 2" x 6' wood	$7.00
One square yard of canvas	$3.50
Nails and glue	pennies
Gesso	$0.50
Latex paint	pennies
Eye screws and wire	pennies

How much have I spent over the last five years building my own canvas stretchers?

Year 1	7 paintings	$80.00
Year 2	12 paintings	$140.00
Year 3	11 paintings	$130.00
Year 4	15 paintings	$175.00
Year 5	11 paintings	$130.00

   If I treat my wife to a steak dinner with a bottle of wine I'll spend more than one hundred dollars. If I treat her on both her birthday and our wedding anniversary, then on an annual basis, I'm spending more money on my wife than my painting. She approves of this.

Invest in your own aesthetic

The evolving aesthetic of Piet Mondrian eventually led him to represent Broadway, the busy avenue in New York City, as a grid of squares and lines. Paul Cezanne painted the mountain Sainte-Victoire more than sixty times in developing his signature aesthetic of planes and volumes. To develop my own aesthetic of painting boats with latex house paint, I set myself the task of doing fifty paintings. Having completed seventeen at this moment, I'm developing a sophisticated understanding of the properties of latex paint, and can anticipate what the background wash will look like, and how to interrupt the flow of the wash in the lower half of the painting to suggest sunlight on water. I've learned how to load my palette knife and then hold it in a certain way so I can incise the edge of a boat on the canvas. I'm beginning to internalize the subtle interaction of palette knife, latex paint and water. Eventually I will possess these phenomena internally and I will be able to paint boat pictures in my imagination, at which point my boat pictures take on a life of their own, growing, changing and morphing in ways that I can't anticipate.

Life is short; art is long precisely because you'll spend your life developing your own aesthetic. If you've ever attempted *plein air* painting, you know how distracting Nature can be and how an internalized aesthetic will help you discover your painting hidden in all of Nature's glorious busyness. Furthermore, if you set up your easel on Dungeness Spit and a troop of girl scouts descends upon you as the most interesting roadside attraction that they've seen so far, they'll ask girl-scout-type questions such as "Are you a real painter?" An internalized aesthetic will help you maintain your focus. This is also true if you set up your easel in Seattle's Fishermen's Terminal to capture the Alaska-bound trawlers and the postprandial strollers on the dock inform you that you've created an uproar in the restaurant just behind because the tourists expected to dine with a panorama of boats, not a painter at work.

But this is *my* discipline to develop *my* aesthetic: this is how I develop *my* skill at painting, a labor of doing fifty paintings. I don't know how you develop *your* aesthetic because that's a private negotiation between you and your talent. How much do you value your talent and how hard are you willing to work to develop your talent? On the other hand, if you're a mere hobbyist, a Sunday painter or *amateur*, or simply seek some amusement in painting and not the labors of Hercules, the art supply marketplace has lots of aesthetics for purchase.

Aesthetics for sale

Pay $29.95 for a DVD that illustrates the Painteasy *(4)* method which empowers you to create beautiful landscapes on your very first try:

> *No experience necessary, you will complete a beautiful oil painting at your very first lesson. Using special firm oil paints for your landscape, and starting with a wet-based canvas, paint glides across the canvas with large brushes. You can make clouds, mountains, trees and water appear in seconds. Beginners will finish a beautiful landscape oil painting at their very first class.*

Occasionally special tools will need to be purchased as well. To do Bob Ross's raccoon painting *(5)* you'll need a wildlife bristle brush, a wildlife detail brush, a wildlife eye brush, etc., as well as the outline of a raccoon to trace.

Frank Clarke's Simply Painting *(2)* reduces landscape painting to the four words "Have Some More Fun," which signify Horizon, Sky, Middle ground and Foreground.

Bill Martin's Guide to Oil Painting *(3)* is built on four exercises and then "you will then have the skills to paint anything you can see or imagine."

Finally, John Beardsworth's *Photoshop: fine art effects cookbook for digital photographers (1)* has a recipe for transforming a photograph of sunflowers into Van Gogh's painting of sunflowers. One of the challenges is creating the swirling blue background of Van Gogh's original, which can be done with the Distort > Twirl tool. The vase in your photograph can be given an artistic look by applying Poster Edges and Paint Daubs effects. The flowers themselves can be antiqued by using Poster Edges because "Van Gogh usually gave every detail an edge." *(1, p. 131)*

Many art supply stores have expanded their business to include craft demonstrations. A mailing brochure informed me that for a mere $124 I can purchase a whole array of styles. It's like shopping for a new hat; I can be an 'old master' this week and an 'abstractionist' next week.

> *We will learn/review the basics of color mixing, temperature and value, glazing and scumbling technique, brush and palette knife use, etc. Students will then receive complete instruction in accomplishing their choice of the following techniques: an Old Masters-style, a traditional oil painting, an Impressionist-style landscape with palette knife, a portrait from a photograph, or an abstract painting.*

If a painter's style is reduced to clicking a button or opening your wallet, then no aspiring painter need be without an aesthetic. The only problem with this path of least resistance is that mechanical tricks, rigid formulae and sausage grinders take every input and output the same meatloaf. If everybody follows the same formula for doing the same arty Van Gogh look-alike, you can expect your viewing audience to be indifferent, heave a sigh, and say "Isn't that the forty-ninth knock-off of Van Gogh I've seen this morning? And did you notice that every detail had an edge?"

I sat on the hard wooden chair in Shepy's office only twice in my life. The first time occurred after he examined my watercolor tests and pronounced that I was ready to move up to the junior painting room. He gave me a small wooden box with six tubes of Grumbacher oil paint with names that were new to me such as Zinc White, Rose Madder, Yellow Ochre and Burnt Umber. I had my wooden paint box under my arm when he presented me to the painting room down the hallway.

Shepy gave us art postcards to copy and every Saturday morning for four years I honed my skill at copying them. *Aesthetics?* I was a prairie boy who didn't use fancy words like that. Art museums were rare on the Canadian prairies during the 1950s, and my awareness of modern art was limited to a book about Norman Rockwell that I borrowed from my school library, and what Life Magazine told me about Jackson Pollock. I had no knowledge of the Impressionists and the name Picasso meant nothing to me. My father gave me and my younger brother a set of biographies of famous American industrialists, as a sort of parental nudge. I remember reading the life story of Henry J. Kaiser who did something with aluminum.

After several years of painting class I developed into a *manically* good copier and arguably the star junior painter. Since the art postcards Shepy asked us to copy were themselves products of a printing process that used black; with work, skill and infinite attention I could make my painting look like a photographed painting that had been produced by a printing process that used black. Both Shepy and his lady assistant were aghast.

The second time that I sat on the hard wooden chair in Shepy's office was when the three of us had a closed-door meeting intended to re-engineer their sorcerer's apprentice with a more socially acceptable aesthetic. Shepy pulled down books of the Impressionists, opened them to the paintings of Monet and pointed at what appeared to be water lilies. "You can't paint just brown," the lady teacher leaned over and whispered in my ear, "Lay in red and green the way the Impressionists do."

I staggered back to my easel and examined the brown tree in the art postcard...no red and green to my eyes, but lots of brown and black. The next week my family moved to Calgary Alberta and my tutelage with Shepy was over. The routine of my life, however, had been set. The next Saturday morning I was in another city, but I assembled my easel in the bedroom that I shared with my brother and sat on the end of my bed looking at him. I had lost my Master, but it was time to paint. I would have to find my own way now.

Develop your own aesthetic

Ultimately, we will all lose our painting Master because it's part of the natural process of developing our own aesthetic. The anxious student who labors to please his painting Master discovers too late that he got it all wrong, that he misunderstood right from the beginning, that it's not just brown he's supposed to be copying, but laying in red and green together. The painting Master is revealed to be an ordinary human being who pulls a book from a shelf and displays Monet's water lilies as a model for emulation.

The only people who can help you are the other souls who, like you, are devoting their lives to becoming painters. Some of them are living and many of them are dead, having lived and created their paintings hundreds of years ago. They are willing to pass along their craft wisdom and you must seize what you can to propel yourself towards your own aesthetic.

Work with a painter
Painting is a complex task that orchestrates your hand, your eye and your brain. If your Master hovers nearby then interventions can be made to adjust your technique. At the end of one class, my mother sat on a chair waiting for me to finish. Shepy interrupted their conversation to correct my grip on my blending brush; that is, he stopped talking to my mother, stood up and walked across the room to adjust my grip on the blending brush. He showed me how to use the side of the blending brush and not the tip, and then he walked back across the room to continue his conversation with my mother.

Painting has a physical dimension beyond language that fuels the master - student relationship. One of my own students was painting water with up and down strokes, and I had to reach out and still his hand. "Move your hand like water," I told him, "Hold the brush like water." Telling someone to move his hand *like water* or to hold a brush *like water* doesn't make rational sense, and illustrates the poverty of words in describing the emotional component of physical actions. I held my student's hand in my hand and together we created the illusion of water by *moving our hands like water*.

Copying originals
Stroll through the galleries of the Louvre and you'll find *artistes copistes* at work. Present yourself to the information desk of the Louvre, under the spectacular I. M. Pei

glass pyramid, and ask for the document *Reglement concernant les conditions de travail des artistes copistes dans les salles et galeries du musee du Louvre.* You can apply for a permit lasting three months that will allow you set up your easel as close as one meter from our object of study. Be careful not to block the view of the tourists and it's forbidden to reproduce the painter's signature.

There is tremendous value in standing close to a masterwork painting. The Seattle Art Museum displayed Bouguereau's *Portrait of Madame la Comtesse de Cambacérès* during 2005 - 2006 and I spent long hours in front of it. Eventually I could distinguish the difference in his strokes in painting the left and right halves of Madame's face. My eye tells me that he was a right-handed painter. If you examine the cream color wood work behind Madame you can see that Bouguereau used a common graphite pencil to darken the contrast of the filigree of the wood work.

Copying reproductions

If you are like the rest of us - you don't live in Paris, France and you're not wealthy enough to finance three months copying at the Louvre - then you are reduced to the poverty of copying from reproductions. You can't hope to capture the original hues because color reproductions are probably several transformations away from the original. That is, a photograph is taken of the original, the photograph is printed in a book, you photocopy the book, etc. I wanted to copy the *Grande Odalisque* by Jean Auguste Dominique Ingres, and gathered a number of books and photocopies only to find that the skin tone of the young lady in the painting varied depending on my reproduction.

Copying a photographic reproduction remains a valuable exercise because you can, at least, come to understand the architecture of a painting. I did a copy of Van Gogh's *The old mill,* and about half way I was exhausted by the high emotion in every element of his painting created by his short, choppy strokes. Copy a painting by Jean-Léon Gérôme to discover a genius of visual architecture. I did a copy of his *Home from the hunt* that shows a hunter on horseback and two dogs in front of a Moorish fountain and drinking pool. I struggled with the delicate Moorish decorations above the pool, the figures in front and to the left of the pool, and as I painted the plants and branches to the right, I recognized that Gérôme had constructed the whole scene to pivot around a big black hole. The casual viewer doesn't see the big black hole. You have to build the painting the way Gérôme did to recognize it.

There is only one way to develop your talent and it doesn't require a lot of dollars. Shut the world out and sit in a corner with a pencil and a paper. Say hello to your visual imagination because you have an appointment with the infinite.

Painting for dollars

It was Sunday morning and I had planted my easel on a hill overlooking Richmond Beach. Sailboats across Puget Sound danced in the sunlight, the Olympic Mountains were majestic in the distance, the green cliffs of Richmond Highlands were to my left and picturesque cottages to my right ornamented the shoreline. A beachcomber wandered far down the beach so I had this beautiful maritime scene with boats, water and mountains all to myself.

But *plein air* painting is harder to do than it sounds and rushing to paint, I had neglected perspective and foreshortening. So the mountains were in the wrong place and this made the curve of the green cliffs wrong. Because I had inadvertently focused too far south, I couldn't fit in any of the cottages. *Frustration!* I decided to switch over to a more expressionist style and slopped some blue paint in the middle of the canvas. *Oh yikes! What a mess.* I was ready to throw the stretcher on the ground when suddenly the beachcomber was at my elbow.

The public tend to ask two questions: "Are you a real painter?" and "How long have you been doing that?" My standard answers are: "I suppose so" and "More than fifty years." He complimented me on how I had captured the scene before us which prompted me to blurted out that I was about to fling the stretcher down the cliff. He was taken aback and urged restraint. "Since you like it, I'll give it to you," I offered.

He was delighted with this idea, "but, put a dog in it, because all good paintings have dogs in them."

"They do?" I asked in amazement. He described the sort of dog he had in mind, and I added a dog walking down the beach. "And I want a bird in the sky." He gave me more instructions about a seagull flying over Puget Sound.

Finally, his painting of water, mountains, beach, dog and seagull was finished. I gave him the painting and he smiled happily, then he ran up the hill towards the parking lot with the painting held high over his head.

Self-actualization: the painter as artist

Hirschman would categorize me as a self-oriented artist: "To follow this course of action requires a great deal of aesthetic or intellectual conviction and may leave the creator with but one satisfied consumer -- the self." *(7, p. 48)*

I paint to please myself and in the happy circumstance that one of my paintings attracts an admirer, I usually give a gift. I gave a copy of a Bouguereau gypsy girl to a neighbor and did the portrait of another neighbor standing in his front yard holding one of his inventions. I portrayed two neighborhood sisters as if they were at the Mad Hatter's tea party and did a dignified portrait of the Dean of my department at the University. These were all gifts. I gave away a boat painting to my son's high school friend. My daughter has several paintings, and when my father died he had several dozen paintings in his home in Arizona. I've done two portraits of my younger brother, my mother wishes that I would paint more flower pictures, my sister-in-law said that "it's nice to have an artist in the family" and my wife advises people that "he can make nice paintings when he wants to." Last summer I sold a painting to a young man named Andre who opened his wallet and gave me his last twelve dollars. I sold a boat painting for five dollars to a former instructor at the Gage Academy of Art who pronounced me "talented" in front of my two grown children and so it goes, day in, day out, etc., being a painter in the 21st century.

The paintings that most interest me are those that strip mine my visual subconscious and selling something so intimate feels odd to me. I like to hang recent work where I can study it. After I have fully absorbed the painting, I either store it or give it away. It's more interesting to find out why people like a painting than just taking their dollars. I like to ask to people, "tell me what you see" and am usually surprised by what they describe. As a painter, you create the thing, but what people make of it will often surprise you.

The beachcomber paid me extravagantly by expressing so much joy when he ran up the hill with my painting.

Marketing: the painter as craftsman

Identifying your target market and fulfilling its needs is the marketing strategy employed by modern merchandisers. (*10, p.12*) The beachcomber got the product he wanted: a dog on the beach and a bird in the sky. When I submitted my creativity to his directions, I became a craftsman; that is, someone who can, on command, portray a dog walking down a beach. A craftsman defines his work as done to meet someone else's practical needs or aesthetic needs. (*1, p.865*)

Paintings are always painted twice, once by the hand of the artist and a second time by the eyes of the beholder. Your patron is re-painting your work as an object that might occupy some space in his world and will trade his dollars for your painting only if the exchange enhances his self-esteem. This is expressed variously in the economics literature as increasing your patron's utility or status or wealth, but basically it's your patron's self-esteem at risk when he considers adding your painting to his world. This is true regardless of the price you ask for your art work. I once offered one of my animal paintings - it was a satire of beach volleyball that pictured two cows in bikinis with a volleyball - to a friend as a gift (cost to her = $0.00). She replied "it's really well done, but I wouldn't want it in my home." Her home represented her self-esteem expressed in worldly goods. Your satiric images might be clever, but if they don't contribute to your patron's self-esteem, you can't even give them away. This fundamental insight into the purchase psychology of the typical art patron suggests two strategies for selling paintings and getting rich quick:

(1) Create images that flatter your target market segment,

(2) Create prestige collectibles that magnify your patron's pride of ownership.

Even the most casual analysis of these two axioms will reveal their similarity: an art purchase is fundamentally an ego purchase, which means that people will buy art only when it enhances their self-esteem. The gap between your self-optimization needs as a painter and the required debasements of flattering your target market segment is yours alone to calibrate, and thereby situate yourself somewhere along the continuum between artist and craftsman. Good luck with any subsequent emotional trauma and identity crisis!

Totem images and the practical uses of flattery
Create a totem image upon which your target market segment can project its ideal self. If you are not familiar with the concept of totem images, visit any magazine shop to discover totem images doing their magic. The front cover of a fishing magazine depicts a huge, finny monster striking a lure, when in reality it's just an eight-inch trout. The fishing

magazine will sell more copies if the front cover emphasizes the ferocity of the trout because fishermen enjoy the conceit of battling monsters rather than scooping minnows. Purchasing a magazine about fishing thus becomes an ego exercise that enhances the self-esteem of the would-be angler.

Many young women both frequent art museums and lead highly charged emotional lives. Certain postcards at the Tate Gallery become totem images as young women project themselves into the role of Ophelia or the Lady of Shalott in the melodrama of their lives:

> *The dreamily romantic style of John William Waterhouse (1849-1917) is seen to great advantage in ... The Lady of Shalott...the intensity of a Pre-Raphaelite vision is muted into a luxuriant and mysterious reverie, a poetic visualization of some of the most loved lines in the English language. The painting vies with Millais's Ophelia for the honour of being the best-selling postcard published by the Tale Gallery. (12, p.459)*

You too can sell to this market segment by sampling women's magazines and finding an emotionally compelling image. Using one of their images would be, of course, leveraging the judgment of the magazine's art director who will have already screened the images for their emotional wattage. Photoshop the image and then expropriate it (i.e., make it your own) by using Filter > Artistic. Here you can find multiple effects such as "colored pencil", "dry brush", "fresco", "neon glow", etc. The path of least resistance would be to project your arty expropriation using an opaque projector and then paint it in a dreamily romantic style. While some small portion of your market segment will reject your painting as disturbing familiar, many more will be reminded of their favorite magazine and gladly give you their dollars. Good luck!

The power of totem images is magnified if your market segment is under competitive stress because group paranoia stimulates the appetite for flattery. Consider the case of the University of Alabama Crimson Tide football team and sports artist Daniel Moore. He bases his paintings on photographs of Alabama football players in heroic action and the many fans of the University of Alabama, gripped by rivalry with the fans of other football teams, have responded enthusiastically:

> *Over the years, Mr. Moore said, his paintings and prints have cumulatively sold "in the low millions." An 8-by-10 reproduction sells for $25 retail or $35 if it is signed. An original watercolor might go for $22,000, an oil for $65,000. (13)*

Any large income stream will attract attention, however, and Moore has been sued by the University of Alabama seeking its fair share. This demonstrates that sometimes painters can be too successful in selling their paintings:

> *In its legal papers, the university's lawyers are grudging in their assessment of Mr. Moore's talent. "Though skillfully prepared," the lawyers wrote, Mr. Moore's art conveys nothing beyond the raw facts of football. Mr. Moore, the suit says, "literally replicates even the expression on the players' faces in his prints and he adds no message whatever not conveyed by the play itself." "That is not fair," Mr. Moore said. Though he uses photographs for reference, he said that his compositions and his style were his own. He calls his approach*

"photofuturism," which he describes as "five parts realism to one part motion." (13)

There are sports teams in every corner of America that would benefit from their own version of photofuturism. Everywhere you go nowadays sports fans are suffering reduced self-esteem. This market segment could easily be enlarged to include any group with self-image stress such as debt collectors, bail bondsmen, professional wrestlers and mortgage bankers (e.g.: Erin Crowe *(27)* did a series of portraits of former Federal Reserve Chairman Alan Greenspan that were eagerly bought by "bankers and hedge-fund people mostly") and don't neglect the owners of certain breeds of dog. The key to creating a totem image for one of these groups is photographing some emotionally charged moment, emphasizing the effect in Photoshop by clever distortion and cropping out anything that doesn't contribute to the heroic action. Once again, use your opaque projector to project the image - unless you've spent years learning how to draw accurately - and paint it up. Good luck!

Any group that has had to hide its identity throughout history will respond enthusiastically to an attractive portrayal. At the first exhibition of the homoerotic drawings of Touko Laaksonen, better known in the gay community as "Tom of Finland," all but one of the drawings were ripped from the walls and stolen. *(23)* This suggests that you should comb the annals of political correctness for the "differently gendered," "differently abled," etc., and create attractive portrayals that will make those folks feel good about themselves. Their gratitude will make you rich and famous.

Groups with tendentious spiritual or religious agendas, who consider themselves at odds with our immoral world, will respond positively to confirmatory images promoting their point of view. Thomas Kinkade uses the visual trope of honey yellow light pouring out the windows of garden cottages to suggest a modern Eden. His glimpses of the Heavenly are prettified with flowers all around.

> *"There's been million-seller books and million-seller CDs. But there hasn't been, until now, million-seller art,"* *says Kinkade. "We have found a way to bring to millions of people, an art that they can understand." (22)*

There probably isn't a home owner anywhere in America who wouldn't respond positively to a painting of his own house with honey yellow light pouring out of the windows. Take a photograph of the house - you won't need a sophisticated image editor for this technique - and replace the front lawn with a mass of wild flowers. Draw over the windows with a yellow fuzz tool. The dollar potential of this strategy has no upside limit if you coordinate with real estate agents and transform their pictures of available homes for sale into glimpses of Eden. That honey yellow light pouring out of the windows looks like gold!

Many people feel themselves to be victims of history and would like to re-write history to their own advantage. It's always flattering to have one's prejudices concerning some historical incident reflected in a painting. For example, the Civil War re-interpretations of Mort Künstler have attracted record crowds.

> *Figures are back lighted with fiery conflagrations, dramatic sunsets and interiors blazing with candles. The proto-cinematic chiaroscuro of late 19th-century academic painting is tweaked to spectral, digital-age levels. Titles are clichéd and sentimental: "Rendezvous*

With Destiny," "Tender Is the Heart" or "War Is Hell!"
(21)

Look around your town for a persecuted racial, religious, linguistic or ethnic minority and transform them from down-trodden victims into high-stepping victors. Critics will accuse you of revisionism, propaganda or being a painter of kitsch, but your nitpickers will be awed when you wave your bank deposit slip high above your head as you stand in queue for the next available teller.

Perhaps the ultimate in totemic flattery would be to picture your patron as the ultimate totem himself, Elvis Presley. The Velvet Store *(25)* transforms a photograph of anyone and re-casts it as Elvis Presley and, furthermore, will do the painting on black velvet.

> *Please keep in mind these are HAND PAINTED by an artist - he can only paint so many hours a day which makes these master pieces even more precious. There are many steps involved in painting on velvet. First the artist will sketch the person (image) to make sure that everything is to scale and accurate. Once the actual painting is started, it is a minimum of 3-5 days per piece as multiple layers of paint are used and each layer has to dry before the next can be added. If we put a time frame on the artist, and rush him, it often jeopardizes the quality. We believe in quality, not quantity. These paintings are true pieces of art! (26)*

Obviously you start with a picture of Elvis Presley, crop out his face and paste in the face of your patron. Project it with your opaque projector, etc. Many fabric stores carry black velvet, but good luck stretching the velvet tight over a wood frame because you don't want to soak the velvet with gesso, the standard technique for shrinking raw canvas to a wood frame. Because this Elvis technique requires messing with a difficult fabric like black velvet, I suggest that you charge extra. Good luck!

Building your painting brand

When your patron stands in front of his latest acquisition, chilled white wine in hand and expansively gestures "this is my Picasso" to his envious friends and fawning admirers, he lives the cliché that Thorstein Veblen *(24)* stigmatized as "conspicuous consumption". The name "Picasso" in this context works as a widely known art brand and adds explosive impact to your patron's status display.

Developing your own brand as painter so that Joe Sixpack recognizes your name, your style of paint application, or your subject matter has been a well-trodden path to commercial success for hundreds of years. One part of brand creation is painting the same thing over and over, or paraphrasing Andy Warhol, "repetition means reputation". *(3)* Betty Parsons, the art dealer, noted the penalty of not restraining yourself to one "marketable artistic signature" in her reflections on the career of Hedda Sterne. Hedda appeared in a group photograph of New York abstract expressionists:

Although the photograph achieved mythic status, and some of its subjects scaled the heights of fame, Ms. Sterne retreated to the margins of art history. She spent the next half-century working steadily at her art and exhibiting frequently, but she never developed a marketable artistic signature. Her frequent stylistic changes, reflecting an exploratory bent, made her an elusive figure. "Hedda was always searching, never satisfied," Betty Parsons, her longtime dealer, once said. "She had many ways; most artists just have one way to go." (6)

Another part of brand creation is creating a public persona that reflects the conventional expectations of behavior that is "arty," "bohemian," "painterly," "creative," etc. We inherit such conventions from branding pioneers such as Gustave Courbet, who in 1850 recognized that he could sell more paintings by manipulating his public image:

> *... in order to publicize the art he undertakes, he needs to be outrageous ("brutal"), a quality that he does not seem to want to confine to his art but that must extend to his whole being, that is, his art and his social behavior, as well as his public statements. (2, p.13)*

Courbet can only be accused of magnifying the personality of the painter in an evolving branding process that increasingly emphasizes the painter at the expense of the painting:

> *From the Restoration period onward, artists such as Delacroix had realized that a reputation was the sine qua non of making sales, and they too had started their careers by submitting to the Salon a succession of "grandes machines" that would make their name. But whereas earlier artists had aimed at critical success and government acquisitions, Courbet's realization ... was that controversy was a faster road to repute than success. (2, p.140)*

The process of promoting the painter at the expense of the painting continues today, although it is increasingly difficult to catch the jaded eye of the potential art patron. Last summer at the Pioneer Square art walk, one young man worked on a canvas lying on the ground and then jumped up to apply paint to his blue jeans and shirt. He crouched again to continue working on the canvas on the ground and then jumped up again to slop more paint on his pants and shirt. The spectacle of a man painting himself began to attract a crowd and he responded to questions by explaining that he had to "get into his painting" and had "to let his body feel the paint," etc. By mid evening he was, in effect, a living painting as he paraded around the square in his wet clothes. He then took out a guitar and sang folk songs to the gawking public. I don't recall that he sold any work, but he certainly attracted more attention than my boat paintings did.

You may despair of ever developing your own brand as a painter, particularly if you like to paint a variety of subjects, and like me, want to keep your clothes clean. Many painters have discovered, however, that the brand itself is their fundamental product and engineer each painting to be just another advertisement for their brand. At this point, the practice of painting gets conceptual.

Giving your painting a conceptual edge

A painting has a concept if it has a story your patron can tell his friends. There are stories that work and stories that don't work. Providing your painting with a good story is not as easy as it sounds. I befriended a young man from the mid-West who was attempting to live on his art sales in Pioneer Square. Things weren't going well for him and he was reduced to using a black felt-tip pen on roofing tiles that he scavenged from the gutter. I witnessed his selling one of them for ten dollars and he immediately abandoned everything to go buy food. (Clichés aside, he really was a *starving* artist.)

   If your patron recounted to his admirers that he paid ten dollars for a discarded roofing tile that had been fetched from the gutter minutes before, and then tarted up with a felt-tip pen, he would be risking ridicule from the more conventionally minded ("*You paid ten dollars for an old roofing tile?*"). Similarly, if your patron told the story of how the artist achieved such an uncanny likeness, some churl might suggest that a photograph could do better. And if your patron exposes his personal taste by appreciating "the deep blue," some cretin might blurt out that "green is the color complement."

   Take a moment to consider the psychological dynamics of your patron's status display and try to create paintings with cachets not so easily challenged as color sense or drawing skill. And, it might be wise to avoid any avant-garde medium such as discarded roof tiles. David W. Galenson *(5)* suggests that conceptual art reigned during the Twentieth Century, and many painters nowadays shield their paintings from critique with a strong conceptual carapace. But take care here too.

   Some painting concepts are so extraordinary that, while they will make your patron's admirers spit up their white wine, they will also overshadow your painting. That is, one remembers the concept and forgets the painting, a state of affairs that will hinder in the long run, especially if your ultimate plan is to sell another painting to your patron next week. In short, what do you do for an encore if your brand consists of the following?

   * Pete Doherty *(15)* paints with his own blood.

   * Tim Patch *(18)* paints with his penis.

* Kieron Williamson *(28)* is only seven years old and is one "of the world's youngest and most internationally known selling artists."

* Elephants, gorillas and monkeys paint at the Louisville Zoo *(17)*.

* Trees can paint *(11)*. (Explanation: tie pens to tree branches and set easels holding paper close by. As the branches sway back and forth in the breeze, the trees "paint", etc.)

My painting master, Professor Shepy, would have recoiled with repugnance at these ghoulish tactics for self promotion. You, too, may shrink with disgust from this circus and seek solace in the quiet pleasures of making beautiful objects. Be forewarned, however, that when you attempt to sell your beautiful objects you will find yourself pitted against whole industries producing wall decor.

The hazards of wall decor
"Wall decor" is a term of contempt for pretty stuff that hangs from the walls. Lots of paintings fall in this category. When you paint with the ambition of prettifying walls, you place yourself in competition with whole industries producing pretty stuff. You will be competing against "wholesale providers of custom framed art & mirrors to the hospitality industry" *(9)* and vendors of posters who have analyzed their market so finely that they can list the eighty seven best selling posters in France. *(4)* Furthermore, your competitors will not be fooling around with handcraft methods, but will employ photo-mechanical processes that can turn out truckloads of wall decor at the flip of a switch. Your competitors will be focused on their "code base."

While experimenting with random noise ...these pictures were made with an applied noise, a random cloud to an elastic brush. I'd like to thank the guys from processing.org and generative-gestaltung.de for providing me such a great code base to experiment with. (14)

Several years ago my mother convinced the owner of a home furnishings store that my paintings were better than the ones he was displaying among his kitchen knickknacks. She phoned me to say that I would have, at last, the opportunity to sell a painting. (*Emotional explanation of this maternal behavior:* both of my parents were chagrined that I had devoted half a century to painting and sold paintings at the rate of about one per decade.) At the time of my mother's phone call, I was studying the problem of background washes by doing a series of flower paintings based on the vases of flowers that my wife set about the house. I had never heard of the store that my mother referred to, and I felt slightly skeptical about the whole process, but to please her we rendezvoused in front of the store and I carried the painting in. The shopkeeper looked it over and then hung it in a dark back room where he stored extra furniture. I remember taking one last look at my painting from the doorway of the room and realized that my painting was nearly invisible in the darkness. I had very low expectations, but it sold within three weeks. *Surprise!*

My mother phoned me with the exciting news that I had, at last, sold a painting. The emotional subtext of our conversation was that the sale had validated fifty years spent painting, and that perhaps I could now move on to something else. The store owner was jubilant as he made out my check, carefully reserving thirty percent for himself. Suddenly richer by several hundreds of dollars, I went through my paintings looking for other flower motifs and found one with yellow lilies. I carried that into the store all by myself, and this time the owner hung it in a front window in the sunshine ... yellow lilies sparkling in the summer sunshine. It, too, sold within three weeks. My head was spinning with this sudden turn of events.

Selling two flower paintings within six weeks threw me into creative turmoil because my visual creative process had moved beyond simple flower paintings with background washes. My angst was magnified by the unfamiliar situation of somebody telling me what to paint. For the previous forty years I had followed my imagination and painted whatever I liked (as long as one lived in Shoreline, one had to be careful of painting *nudes*, of course). One of the advantages of being ignored by the marketplace is the freedom to paint whatever you wished. Now I was faced with the opportunity to make big bucks, if I could only paint flower pictures, but my visual imagination demanded that I add birds flying in and amongst blooms. (Aesthetic note: I draw nearly everything from my imagination so that, while my birds are not cartoon birds, they don't look like the birds of Audubon either. My birds are *my* birds.) I was caught between the demands of the marketplace and the demands of my visual imagination. I was stuck.

I carried in my painting of a blue bird flying winging its way through flowers. The shopkeeper used it as background for a display of knives, forks and flatware, then he tried it as the background of a sofa/lamp combination, and then he finally parked it about twelve feet up in the air on top of a display cabinet of imported South American table clothes and napkins. You had to back up across the shop and crane your neck to see it. After six months I retrieved it and he commented as I carried it out, "glad to see the birdie go." My feelings were hurt. Several weeks later I offered him some other paintings, but he refused to accept them in his shop because "they're the wrong color." He had shifted to an autumn theme in his shop and my paintings weren't autumnal colors.

I don't do paintings based on trendy or seasonal colors. Proprietors of home decor shops sell candles, glassware, cushions, and so on, and any paintings that they sell are commodities just like this season's table napkins. The proprietor eventually found someone who did paintings of pears -- red ones, blue ones, yellow ones, big ones and little ones, paintings of two pears and paintings of three pears, pears lined up in a row and pears in a column, etc. "We sell a lot of those," he told me. My visual imagination doesn't suggest an endless series of pear images, unfortunately. A blue bird ended my career as the decorator of kitchen walls. My mother loves the painting of the blue bird and the flowers, however, and has it hanging over her kitchen table.

Be a painter or a craftsman, but not both

Stand on any street corner in America and critically examine the passing crowd - your future art patrons are parading before you. Who are these people to whom you offer the products of your unique and most heart-felt creativity and from whom you expect to receive dollars?

* They're stressed-out, over-caffeinated, digitally titillated and have developed a defensive reflex to prevent their eyeballs from being hijacked by the screaming media around them. You got another image called a painting? Please, they're busy. Call back some other time.

* You want money for your paintings? Your future art patrons are swamped with free images thanks to our in-your-

face advertising culture, and furthermore, even if you were able to catch their attention, they don't have discretionary dollars to give you. The Pew Center reports *(19)* that fewer Americans than ever can maintain a middle-class lifestyle. Let me put that more bluntly: your art patrons need food and shelter, not your paintings. Buying art is an ego purchase; buying potatoes is a calorie purchase. Guess which one comes first.

* The average American - your future art patrons - is challenged to distinguish a Manet from a Monet. A scholarly survey of arts education *(29)* declares that institutional support for any kind of arts education is weak with the consequence that

> ...*Americans may have to abandon the ideal of democratized arts and acknowledge that the arts are going to become, like literacy in an earlier age, largely the province of the educated elite. (29, p. 102)*

Web sites such as *Mental_floss* (www.mentalfloss.com) are coming to the rescue of Americans who embarrass themselves by confusing Monet and Manet:

> *Take a step closer to the painting. If you're looking at tiny dabs of paint working together to create a landscape, chances are you've got a Monet in front of you. If, on the other hand, you're looking at loosely painted images of chubby Parisians, you're probably staring at a Manet. (16)*

You are driven by a visual subconscious towards personal growth and the development of a unique personal aesthetic? This probably means you're a member of the cultural elite and the avant-garde. Pause to reflect on the relationship between the popular taste of the American art-buying public and the avant-garde of your personal vision. Robert Hughes would label the no man's land between the two as "shock of the new":

> *The essence of the avant-garde myth is that the artist is a precursor; the truly significant work of art is the one that prepares the future. (8, p. 366)*

Given that your future art patrons lack a basic arts education, an essential for appreciating any aesthetic innovation, what kind of reception would you expect from the novelties you present them?

Your fantasy is to self-actualize by putting marks on paper and have people give you their dollars? Very few people have ever been in that sweet spot. Ad Reinhardt described the New York art scene during the 1960s:

> *Now almost every artist outside of New York is connected with some school or some museum school and even in New York the majority are. That's an interesting fact when you take the idea of making money, making a living selling paintings. Only a dozen or two painters do that. [20, p. 24]*

Be a painter and live a life that is a reproach to the crass commercialism of our stunted age. Make aesthetic objects that the passing herd can't comprehend and that have no apparent market value. Go into a corner and draw fifty boat pictures from your imagination just to enlarge your personal creativity and gain spiritual refreshment, just don't expect to get rich doing it.

Famous paintings and famous painters

You may be impatient with the gentle rewards of painting: how a tight canvas responds like a living membrane to the pressure of a brush, or the *oh-my-gosh* moment when you seek a special hue by driving a knife through several pigments to rainbow them across your palette.

You may be annoyed when the spotlight of notoriety - *not fame* - suddenly shines on you. I was portraying the ferries coming and going in Mukilteo when a woman ran out of a restaurant exclaiming that she loved painters more than her boyfriend. There was some unpleasantness when her boyfriend caught up with her and saw what I was doing. I was in the middle of an Impressionist rendering of the boats moored along the dock of the old Waterfront Activity Center at the University of Washington when a guy with a camera suddenly leaped out of the bushes behind me and caught me mid-stroke. He explained that he was photographing exotic local types and I replied that stalking people through the underbrush was pretty exotic too.

Getting my easel and canvas down to the Burke-Gilman trail along Lake Washington meant lashing them to the back of my bicycle and yes, it did resemble an airplane contraption, but passing bicyclists commenting that "the Wright brothers started out that way" were gratuitous and cruel. *What has happened to the 19th-century spirit of hiking out to do a painting of Mont Sainte-Victoire?* My family called it the "artmobile" which was just harmless family joshing. But when the artmobile broke down (I lost a screw in the bike rack over the rear wheel and the leg of the rack was jammed through the spokes of the rear wheel), it was hurtful when a bystander, before lending me his cell phone to call for rescue, wanted to know if I was a serial murderer. *The modern world can't distinguish painters from serial murderers! What next?*

Perhaps you disdain such misadventures of notoriety - *not fame* - and hanker after a more exalted renown for you and your paintings.

Making a famous painting

Fame means a lot of people know. An unknown master of centuries ago paints a mural in a church and generations of adherents supplicate before it. That anonymous master created a successful image because many people recognize it, worship it, cherish it and chart their lives by it. In the modern age a similar fame can be manufactured by advertising. Fischer *(10)* reported that nearly 30% of 3-year-old children and 90% of 6-year-old children in 1991 could recognize "Old Joe" - the camel who smokes cigarettes. The ethics of promoting smoking to children aside, "Old Joe" is a famous image.

A few paintings, however, surpass mere high recognition - *the truly famous paintings* - morph into memes *(8),* cultural fragments that people commandeer and re-purpose. Leonardo da Vinci painted the portrait of a young woman and Marcel Duchamp adorned her with a mustache, a meaningless conceptual jape had not the *Mona Lisa* already evolved into a cultural icon, recognized by millions and carrying a cultural meaning that Duchamp could subvert. A Google Image search for "Mona Lisa" returns more than three millions images, most of them parodies. "Mona Lisa", the song, won an Academy Award in 1950. That's fame.

If Leonardo's *Mona Lisa* or Michelangelo's *Creation of Adam* are out of your league, ponder Grant Wood's *American Gothic* which won third place in a competition in 1930, and was then bought by The Art Institute of Chicago for a mere $300. *(3)* On December 24, 1934 it was widely distributed for the first time in Time Magazine and the public immediately responded.

> *American Gothic remains one of the most famous paintings in the history of American art...The painting has become part of American popular culture, and the couple has been the subject of endless parodies. (12)*

A Google Image search for "American Gothic" returns 2.6 million hits. That's fame.

It's yet another Monday morning in the lumpy saga of your life as a painter, and sipping your third coffee, you pine for some lodestone to guide you. No problem. Drop your coffee, pull out your easel and aim to do better than Grant Wood. That is, create an image that millions will embrace, parody endlessly, and proudly wear on T-shirt and ball cap. If you don't quite succeed on Monday, try again on Tuesday, and keep going until you succeed. Simple goals are often the really tough ones and this one might take longer than you think.

You're on your death bed and despite your blinding cataracts you spy a hospice nurse wearing a ball cap adorned with one of your paintings; die easy; you've made a famous painting.

They call you a famous painter

You take an evening stroll across the Piazza San Marco in Venice and the whispering crowd parts before you and carried aloft in the evening air are the sweet words you covet:

"there goes a famous painter!" Suppose I pedal the artmobile past you at that moment and the crowd recoils in shrieking self defense. Their verbal acts have transformed you into a famous painter and me into a traffic hazard. John Searle's analysis of "status function declarations" *(21)* suggests that the social status of "famous painter" is a verbal construct: you become a famous painter when others call you a famous painter. Being a famous painter is not an absolute personal attribute such as your thumb print or eye color, but a social attribute given to you by the speech acts of other people:

> *But notice how the language that we use to describe these phenomena functions. It creates them. The language constitutes them in an important way. Why? Because the phenomena in question are what they are in virtue of being represented as what they are. The representations, which are partly constitutive of institutional reality, the reality of government, private property, and marriage as well as money, universities and cocktail parties, is essentially linguistic. Language doesn't just describe; it creates, and partly constitutes, what it both describes and creates. (21, p. 85)*

You may wear a beret and look like a famous painter; you can set up your easel and wave a brush around in the air. So far you're just a painter, i.e., somebody who paints. If the passing spectators don't engage in the verbal complicity of calling you a famous painter, you're not a famous painter.

Dealing with a lack of recognition is always frustrating, but consider the difficulty of molding public opinion. First, differences of opinion are rife ("He's a famous painter!" "Do you really think so?"), and the connoisseurs of painting are famously feckless ("Last year I thought he was a famous painter, but that was last year"). Getting yourself hailed as a famous painter is difficult because the verbal behavior of other people is largely beyond your control. Good luck!

Art critics call you a famous painter

Art critics are intellectuals who construct narratives explaining art, its origins, development and social meaning. While these narratives can be flavored differently (e.g.: "Impressionist", "Pre-Impressionist", "Post-Impressionist", "Modern", "Pre-Modern", "Post-Modern", etc.) they all tend to impose order upon chaos by lining painters up, grouping them thematically and casting them as actors in the critic's compelling story. Art critics are sophisticated enough to invent the category "outsider art" for oddments that don't quite fit.

Art critics are never happier than when they can show time's arrow delineating the history of painting as an orderly narrative with a beginning, middle and end. Here the art reviewer of *The New York Times* slots George Condo into art history to create such a grand march:

> *He's the missing link, or one of them (Carroll Dunham is another), between an older tradition of fiercely loony American figure painting — Willem de Kooning's grinning women, Philip Guston's ground-meat guys, Jim Nutt's cubist cuties, anything by Peter Saul — and the recent and updated resurgence of that tradition in the work of Mr. Currin, Glenn Brown, Nicole Eisenman, Dana Schutz and others. (7)*

Thus this art critic adorns George Condo with the status of famous painter. Your likely ignorance of George Condo, as well as the other names in this narrative, merely indicates its arbitrary and obscure nature.

I haven't met any art critics, and I imagine that you haven't either. I recommend that you consider being called a famous painter by an art critic as a low-probability event. First, you would have to find one and then initiate a campaign to elicit the specific verbal behaviors from him or her that would result in the appellation "famous painter." Good luck!

Your obituary calls you a famous painter

I'm morbidly attracted to reading the life stories of painters which conveniently arrive at my breakfast table in the form of the obituaries of *The New York Times*. I eat my porridge each morning and parse the stunning triumphs and gruesome defeats of recently dead painters.

I also love reading art histories and I happen to have two of them close at hand right now: *History of modern art* by H.H. Arnason (2004) and *Art today* by Edward Lucie-Smith (1999). The puffery on the cover of the first calls it "comprehensive, authoritative and insightful," qualities you would expect in a textbook my daughter read in an introductory art survey course at the university. The other book bills itself as the "definitive source of information on the art of the modern era."

Ever wonder how many people have an obituary describing them as an important, influential or beloved painter, but then are ignored by histories of art billing themselves as "comprehensive" and "definitive"? You might choke on your porridge.

Here's a five-year survey of obituaries dated sufficiently long ago to have given Arnason and Lucie-Smith plenty of time to write them up.

1987 Ben Stahl (died October 24, 1987) published 750 illustrations in *The Saturday Evening Post* and was hailed as a "master" by Norman Rockwell. *(24)* Raphael Soyer (died November 5, 1987) was "America's leading advocate of realism" *(23)*. Anton Pieck (died November 28, 1987) "created scenes that have appeared on millions of Christmas cards," *(19)* and finally, Minnie Evans (died December 19, 1987) became "one of the best known of black American folk artists." *(9)*

 None of these painters appear in Arnason or Lucie-Smith. Imagine the millions of people who have seen one of Stahl's illustrations or sent one of Pieck's Christmas cards. If fame is based on the number of people who know your images, these are famous painters. *My goodness!*

 1988 Neil Williams (died March 30, 1988) pioneered the use of the shaped canvas. *(30)* Patrick Hogan (died May 9, 1988) "achieved renown as a painter in Los Angeles despite a handicap that allowed him only the use of his mouth to hold a paintbrush." *(14)* The British Museum recently bought the entire collection of graphic work done by Stanley William Hayter (died May 6, 1988) during the years 1926 to 1960. *(13)* Finally, Primo Conti (died November 13, 1988) was the last major surviving figure of Italy's futurist school of painting. *(6)*

 None of these painters appear in Arnason or Lucie-Smith. Hogan had to hold a brush in his mouth and I feel sorry for myself because my hand trembles occasionally! Imagine having the British Museum collect your total corpus. *My goodness!*

 1989 Millard Sheets (died April 4, 1989) is represented in forty-six museums. *(22)* John Ford Clymer (died November 4, 1989) painted more than eighty covers for the *Saturday Evening Post* between 1945 and 1963. *(5)*

 Neither of these painters appears in Arnason or Lucie-Smith. Imagine having your work represented in forty-six museums while I haven't been able to wedge a single painting into even one museum. *My goodness!*

1990 Affandi (died May 25, 1990) was "Indonesia's foremost expressionist painter." *(1)* Ralph Humphrey (died July 17, 1990) was famed for "a deep yet bright blue, full of intimations of red" *(15)* and was considered a link between Abstract Expressionism and Minimalism. The obituaries of Jan Stussy (died August 2, 1990) *(25)* and Marguerite Wagstaff (died October 17, 1990) *(29)* report that each painter created more than 5,000 paintings. At the height of her career in the 1950's and 1960's, the paintings of Ann Cole Phillips (died December 16, 1990) were compared to Kandinsky, Dufy and Kokoschka. *(18)*

None of these painters appear in Arnason or Lucie-Smith. Suppose that you complete one hundred paintings per year and continue in this fashion for fifty years. That is 5,000 paintings. A search for "Jan Stussy" on Google Images returns examples of his work, but a search for "Marguerite Wagstaff" returns no images of paintings. Spend a lifetime producing five thousand paintings and no trace is left. How about being compared to Kandinsky, Dufy and Kokoschka? *My goodness!*

1991 Elmer Bischoff (died March 6, 1991) was a pioneer of the Bay Area figurative school of painting. Along with the painters Richard Diebenkorn and David Park, he broke with abstraction and began to work in the powerful style that later became known as Bay Area figurative painting. *(4)* Rufino Tamayo (died June 25, 1991) joined the three great Mexican muralists Diego Rivera, Jose Clemente Orozco and David Alfaro Siqueiros to bring international attention to 20th-century Mexican art. *(26)*

Neither of these painters appears in Arnason or Lucie-Smith. Imagine having your name mentioned in the same sentence with Richard Diebenkorn or Diego Rivera. *My goodness!*

Now finish your porridge.

Grocery stores call you a famous painter

I discovered the work of Andrew Wyeth, a painter who astonishes me with his brushwork, in a grocery store in Alberta during the 1960s. At the time, selling art prints in grocery stores was a marketing novelty. My mother picked through the cabbages and I leafed through Wyeth.

It's a sort of fame...the prairie farmers of Alberta, dressed in boots and parkas, pushing their shopping carts around the vegetable display and stumbling upon Wyeth's *Christina's World*, a painting depicting a woman crawling across the prairie towards a distant house.

You're a truly famous painter when your work sells alongside vegetables.

An art gallery calls you a famous painter

Getting a show in an art gallery is hard! I've walked into galleries and asked about submitting slides. A nice young lady sitting at the front counter of an art gallery in Seattle once told me that I should put them in an envelope and send them in, but she indicated that it would be a waste of time. There was a pile of brown envelopes about two feet high behind the counter - "it would go onto the slush pile." She confided that she was a painter as well, and her strategy for insinuating a painting or two into the gallery was by working the front desk.

Getting a show in an art gallery is easy! Securing a one-man show was as easy as having dinner in a Thai food restaurant with the gallery owner. A friend recommended me to him; then we all had dinner together. I brought along some prints and the gallery manager liked them, and within minutes I was on their schedule for a month-long, one-man show.

Had I suddenly become an art world insider? Sensing a big break or a turning point in my painting career, I bought advertising in the local newspaper and sent invitations to the local art critics. To complement the paintings on the walls, I made some postcard-sized prints to sell as well. Opening night I had a crowd of family, students and colleagues, and two of my students bought prints. While I chatted with the crowd, the gallery owner and his manager sat behind the cash register in the next room, waiting. None of the paintings sold. Nothing sold all month. When I went to pick up my paintings, the gallery owner was sorely disappointed: "they didn't exactly fly off the walls," he said bitterly and reminisced that a recent show by another painter had sales of more than $1,000.

The drama of your life as a famous painter

The sociologist Erving Goffman *(11)* suggests that the drama of everyday life will inform spectators that you're a painter. The "drama of everyday life" simply means whatever you do in the public eye. Set your easel up in public and, based on my experience, people will ask "are you a painter?"

When Ford Madox Brown was painting *Work*, his image of workers digging up a road, which symbolically challenged the social fabric of Victorian England, he constructed a painting wagon that he pushed through the streets. "Local children thought it promised a Punch and Judy show, as he wheeled it daily through the Hampstead streets." *(27, p. 95)* Stanley Spencer used an old baby pram in his village of Cookham to move his painting equipment about. Spencer was a visionary who was so deeply immersed in his inspiration that he was unaware of the spectacle he created.

There is a photo *(17, p. 49)* of Spencer doing quick sketches on toilet paper in the shipyards on the Clyde. You're a no-nonsense welder who slams metal all day and then you halt work while painter sketches you on toilet paper that unrolls across the dock. Stanley Spencer attained the moniker of "famous painter" that day among the shipwrights on the Clyde.

Maud Lewis (1903 - 1970), the Nova Scotia folk artist, turned her house into her gallery. She painted on the walls, cupboard doors, cookie sheets and so on. Her little house is preserved at the Art Gallery of Nova Scotia in Halifax. Henry Darger (1892 - 1973), the outsider artist in Chicago, filled a second-floor room on Chicago's North Side, at 851 W. Webster Avenue, with his art. Your home becomes your gallery informing the public that you're a painter:

> *The artists' houses that grew up in late 19th-century London were an integral part of the economics of the late Victorian art world. They were built for entertaining and impressing patrons as much as for painting or living in. They acted as a discreet shop window for an artist's work: but the role of the studio was more subtle than simply as a place to sell pictures, a function which could also be undertaken at an art dealer's gallery or a public exhibition. The studios were lavishly contrived to show off the artists' taste in decoration and objets d'art as well as to display their own paintings. The effect was to enhance the status of the painters as cultural and social arbiters, and thus to increase the desirability of owning an example of their work. (28)*

Anonymous was a famous painter

Ad Reinhardt has the last word about famous painters:

> *The early Chinese painters are legendary "heroes," often anonymous, often with several names, often with no existing or even ever known works of art. Western museums are so full of stuff that exists that it is refreshing to think about paintings that do not exist. (20, p. 213-4)*

Paintings live and die

I build with wood sticks and raw canvas, nails and staples, a delicate rectangular frame that holds a slack canvas. I take it to my gesso station in the carport for the birth of another stretcher. The magic begins when I sop the dry canvas with gesso and water: the stretcher comes to life as the canvas shrinks and hugs its wooden skeleton. I stroke the water and gesso left and right, up and down and rotate the canvas to even the flow of wetness. Bugs land on the wet surface and pine needles carried by the wind stick to it. Your painting is a thing of nature. By varying the amounts of water and gesso, I can make this new child thin and tight, or loose and fat. Sometimes the force of the shrinkage will twist the side boards and pull the corners apart. If I've been lazy and haven't braced the sides sufficiently, or stapled carelessly; I birth a deformed child with lumpy stapled corners or even worse, sides that bow inwards. How does one treat a deformed child? Should I invest my inspiration on an imperfect stretcher, where people will say *"what a nice painting,"* but every time I look at it I can see the curve sides? *Anguish!*

A painting is a real object that lives in the material world. Dust will pile up on the top edge, the cotton will rot, the wood frame will crack and anything that touches the painted surface changes it.

> *Although as an image the Last Supper enjoys an exceptional fame, the painting, like any work of art, is*

composed of physical substances which are subject to
damage and decay. The mural began to deteriorate, in
fact, during Leonardo's lifetime. (1)

I always alert people to carry a painting by the wooden frame and not to press against the painted surface. But when I'm driving on the freeway, my van sways left and right, and behind me I can hear my paintings shifting position, a whole rack of paintings acting in concert, falling from one side of the van to the other. I had arranged them in the van so carefully, bracing one against the wooden frame of the others so as to protect the painted surfaces. When I arrive and take them out of the van, I can see the damage as shallow ripples in the painted surfaces. Is it possible that I am both the prime creator and destroyer of my own paintings?

I have so many paintings that I store them in our crawl space. The dirt floor of the crawl space is damp so I built a wooden platform to keep them dry. Eventually, my storage is full and I have to make decisions about which paintings to kill. To take a painting off its stretcher and then roll it up in a large roll with dozens of others is effectively to kill it. Once a canvas has been rolled, it won't lay flat again, and since each stretcher that I build is unique, the canvas would be very difficult, perhaps impossible to stretch again.

I've murdered paintings. I've abandoned paintings that I don't like on the back deck during a wet Seattle winter and watched the green scum grow on them. Paintings rot and return to the earth. I've left paintings out by the garden shed and when time comes to rip them apart, there are spiders living in the stretcher in the folds of canvas.

Since I don't sell many paintings, I've tried giving them away. I once prepared a small sign that read "Free" that I intended to attach to a painting, and then set the painting against a tree at a discrete distance from the busy part of the Art Walk. My plan was to unobtrusively monitor interest in the painting among the passersby, and if someone stopped to admire it, offer it to this person as a gift. But a Seattle city official monitoring the art walk saw the sign, and admonished me about the requirement to sell art at the art walk: "If you give away paintings, nobody will be able to sell," she told me.

I removed the sign. It's even difficult to give paintings away. Later that evening, however, I did convince a couple that the painting was free and that they could have it. People don't understand how a painter could give away a painting, *"you could sell this for hundreds of dollars"* they say to me, but they accept the gift. How many people have discretionary funds of hundreds of dollars for buying a painting at an art walk? Occasionally I see the couple again and ask about my painting. It's an orphan child in a new home; I have the impulse to ask them "how is my baby that you've adopted?"

My daughter was moving from one apartment to another in Bellingham and we left some of my paintings on the front lawn of the house for passersby to pick up. Several months later, she was at a party in the same neighborhood and found one of those abandoned paintings hanging in the bathroom of the party house. There must be half a dozen of my paintings scattered around and moving from student house to student house in Bellingham right now.

About a decade ago the Arts Council of Shoreline contacted me about lending a painting to my legislative representative's office in Olympia. I carried over a still life of two oranges and the painting has never returned to me. Somewhere in Olympia my still life is living its own life. In Seattle, Bellingham and Olympia people are living with my paintings and they have no way to link them back to me. I suppose that it makes me an anonymous master.

"We come to painting, to poetry, to the stage, hoping to revive the soul. And any artist whose work touches us earns our gratitude... it is when art acts as an agent of transformation that we may correctly speak of it as a gift. (2, p. 59)

I exhibited a painting called "The circularity of the hydrology cycle" at the Shoreline Arts Festival. Several weeks later I received a telephone call from a woman whose deceased husband had been a hydrologist. She recognized the word "hydrology" in the title of the painting, and wanted to see the painting. The painting touched her emotionally and I should have given it to her as a gift, but I still had ambitions of selling my paintings. I told her that I wanted to sell if for four hundred dollars, but she was a widow living on social security and didn't have money like that to spend on a painting.

For the last several years the painting has been stored in my crawl space. I regret not giving it to her. What better thing to do than make something that another person cherishes and then give it as a gift?

Did I ever paint fifty boat pictures?

My meticulous reader will wonder if I am as disciplined as I claim to be; that is, did I succeed in painting fifty boat pictures using latex house paint and a palette knife?

Well, no.

I got up into the mid 20s and then Autumn Quarter started at the university and my life got busy. During the Christmas holidays I saw some amazing photographs of the snowy winter in Europe and I did about a dozen cityscapes, which boosted my total of latex paintings into the high 30s. Winter quarter was another busy ten weeks for me, but while it was cold and rainy in Seattle, I began a virtual tour of the coast of France via Google Earth viewing both photographs and 3D imagery. More than one hundred years after Monet stood on the cliffs of Fécamp, I could too.

> *At the fishing port of Fécamp, Monet begins a group of coastscapes, realizing subjects that he has prospected during the winter of 1868-69. Assuming viewpoints on the coastal clifftops as well as on the beaches, Monet addresses vast barren spaces with activated stenographic brushwork suggesting the tossing sea. (1, p. 206)*

With my little art boards and my latex house paint, I began to portray the ports and fishing villages of France. Once, in January, my paint froze before it dried. I'm past fifty latex paintings now and have ordered more boards to paint on. I never did complete fifty boat pictures, but my house-paint aesthetic is growing more sophisticated weekly. Buy me a coffee and I can tell you how to paint a picture of the Brittany coast in latex house paint.

The arc of growth and development of my latex aesthetic is about completed because my visual imagination tickled me this morning with the idea of an oil painting of a little girl dancing in a circle with a dinner plate and a spoon. *Hmmm, I'll have to play with that idea.* Perhaps it's time to move on to other delights.

REFERENCES

Caught unawares by the 19th century
1. "About colors in digital graphics" Adobe Community Help. *Using Illustrator CSS* (last updated 2/25/2010): p. 115.
2. Ackerman, Gerald M. *The life and work of Jean-Léon Gérôme with a catalog raisonne.* Sotheby's Publications, 1986.
3. Beardsworth, John. *Photoshop Fine Art Effects Cookbook.* O'Reilly, 2006.
4. DeviantART blog. Posted Tuesday August 17, 2010. http://hq.deviantart.com/blog/
5. "Jackson Pollock: Is he the greatest living painter in the United States?" *Life Magazine*, August 8, 1949.
6. Koschmann, Timothy, Kari Kuutti and Larry Hickman. "The Concept of Breakdown in Heidegger, Leont'ev, and Dewey and Its Implications for Education." *Mind, Culture, and Activity* 5 (1), 1998.
7. "Let's Play Llama Trading Game!" A deviantART announcement. http://hq.deviantart.com/blog/31326194/

Drawing your inner vision
1. Bell, Julian. "Desire of the line." *The Times Literary Supplement*, No. 5624 (January 14, 2011)
2. Bruce, Vicki, Elias Hanna, Neal Dench, Pat Healey, and Mike Burton. "The importance of 'mass' in line drawings of faces." *Applied Cognitive Psychology*, 6 (1992): 619-628.
3. Gayford, Martin. *Man with a blue scarf: on sitting for a portrait by Lucian Freud.* London: Thames & Hudson, 2010.

4. Hockney, David. *Secret knowledge: Rediscovering the lost techniques of the old masters.* Studio, 2006.

5. Quantrill, Mike. "Drawing as a gateway to computer human integration." *Leonardo*, 35 (February 2002).

6. Rockwell, Norman. *Rockwell on Rockwell: How I make a picture.* New York: Watson-Guptil, 1979.

7. Ross, Bob. "Painting supplies." Accessed June 25, 2010. http://www.bobross.com/Supplies.cfm

8. Salvador, Ana. *Draw with Pablo Picasso.* Frances Lincoln Children's Books, 2008.

Reading "Art and Fear"

1. Bayles, David and Ted Orland. *Art & fear: observations on the perils (and rewards) of artmaking.* Santa Barbara: Capra Press, 1993.

2. Goldhaber, Michael H. "The attention economy hypothesis in brief" Accessed July 2010. http://goldhaber.org/blog/?p=197

3. "Hirst sells skull for $100 million, manager says." Accessed March 2011. http://www.bloomberg.com/apps/news?pid=newsarchive&sid=alrptIf1av3g&refer=muse

4. Hulsker, Jan. *The new complete Van Gogh: paintings, drawings, sketches.* Amsterdam: J. M. Meulenhoff, 1996.

5. King, Ross. *The judgment of Paris: the revolutionary decade that gave the world Impressionism.* New York: Walker, 2006.

6. jQuery. Accessed March 2011. http://sixrevisions.com/ resources/14-jquery-plugins-for-working-with-images/

7. Life Magazine. "Picasso" December 27, 1968.

8. Lucie-Smith, Edward. *Art today.* London: Phaidon Press, 1995.

Dollars for painting
1. Beardsworth, John. *Photoshop: Fine art effects cookbook for digital photographers.* O'Reilly, 2006
2. Clarke, Frank. "Simply Painting" Accessed January 2011. http://www.simplypainting.com/
3. Martin, Bill "Oil painting lessons" Accessed January 2011. http://www.guidetooilpainting.com/
4. Painteasy. Accessed January 2011. http://www.painteasy.com/a_landscapes.html
5. Ross, Bob. "Raccoon" http://www.bobross.com /howto2.cfm?type=Wildlife&Page=Raccoon&ExpandHowTo= True

Painting for dollars
1. Becker, Howard. "Arts and crafts." *American Journal of Sociology,* 83 (January 1978): 862-889.
2. Chu, Petra ten-Doesschate. *The most arrogant man in France: Gustave Courbet and the Nineteenth-Century media culture.* Princeton University Press, 2007.
3. Churchwell, Sarah. "Too many Marilyns." *The Guardian,* Tuesday 29 May 2007. http://www.guardian.co.uk/ commentisfree/2007/may/29/film.comment
4. "France's best sellers." Accessed January 2011. http://www.allposters.com/-st/France-s-Best-Sellers-Posters_c86393_.htm
5. Galenson, David W. *Conceptual revolutions in Twentieth-century art.* Cambridge University Press, 2009.
6. Grimes, William. "Hedda Sterne, an artist of many styles, dies at 100" *New York Times,* April 11, 2011.
7. Hirschman, Elizabeth C. "Aesthetics, ideologies and the limits of the marketing concept." *Journal of Marketing,* 47 (Summer 1973): 45-56.

8. Hughes, Robert. *The shock of the new*. Knopf, 1981.

9. "Images for your walls." Accessed February 2011. http://www.imagesforyourwalls.com/

10. Kotler, Philip and Gary Armstrong. *Principles of Marketing*. Prentice Hall, 1991

11. Knowles, Tim. "Tree drawings." Accessed January 2011. http://www.timknowles.co.uk/ Work/TreeDrawings/ tabid/265/Default.aspx

12. Lambourne, Lionel. *Victorian painting*. Phaidon Press, 1999.

13. Liptak, Adam. "Sports artist sued for mix of crimson and tide" *The New York Times*, November 12, 2006.

14. Maeder, Michael T. "Framed art for hotels." Accessed January 2011. http://www.framedartforhotels.com/ new-the-agent-series/

15. Mendick, Robert. "Doherty's blood paintings. " *The Evening Standard*. Accessed January 2011. http://www.thisislondon.co.uk/showbiz/article-22525591-details/ + Doherty%27s+blood+paintings/article.do

16. "Mental_floss, where knowledge junkies get their fix." Accessed February 2011. http://www.mentalfloss.com/ difference/monet-vs-manet/

17. "New zoo store sells paintings done by animals." Accessed February 2011. http://www.bizjournals.com/louisville/ stories/2009/05/04/daily59.html

18. Patch, Tim. "Have penis, will paint." Accessed December 2010. http://news.softpedia.com/ news/ Have-Penis-Will-Paint-31238.shtml

19. Pew Research Center. "Inside the middle class." Accessed November 2010. http://pewresearch.org/pubs/793/inside-the-middle-class

20. Reinhardt, Ad. *Art-as-art: The selected writings of Ad Reinhardt,* edited and with an introduction by Barbara Rose. University of California Press, 1975

21. Schwendener, Martha. "Applying broad strokes to a time of war." *The New York Times*, October 8, 2010

22. "Thomas Kinkade: a success." Accessed November 2010. http://www.cbsnews.com/stories/ 2001/11/21/ 60minutes/main318790.shtml

23. "Tom of Finland: a short biography." Accessed November 2010. http://www.tomoffinlandfoundation.org/ foundation/touko.html

24. Veblen, Thorstein. *Theory of the leisure class.* Project Gutenberg e-book 833.

25. The Velvet Store. Accessed October 2010. http://www.thevelvetstore.com/Merchant2/merchant.mv

26. The Velvet Store. "Custom Elvis makeover." Accessed September 2010. http://www.thevelvetstore.com/Merchant2/ merchant.mv? Screen=CTGY&Store_Code=vs02&Category_Code=13

27. Vinzant, Carol. "Mona Lisa of the Federal Reserve." *New York Magazine,* January 28, 2006. http://nymag.com/ news/intelligencer/15642/

28. Williamson, Kieron. "Homepage" http://www.kieronwilliamson.com/

29. Zakaras, Laura and Julia F. Lowell. *Cultivating demand for the arts: arts learning, arts engagement and state art policy.* Rand corporation, 2008.

Famous paintings and famous painters

1. Affandi. [Obituary] http://www.nytimes.com/1990/ 05/25/obituaries/affandi-painter-83.html?scp=1& sq=obituary +painter&st=nyt

2. Arnason, H. H. *History of modern art: painting, sculpture, architecture, photography.* Prentice-Hall, 2004.

3. Biel, Steven. *American Gothic: A Life of America's Most Famous Painting.* W. W. Norton & Company, 2005.

4. Bischoff, Elmer. [Obituary] http://www.nytimes. com/1991/03/06/obituaries/elmer-bischoff-west-coast-painter-is-dead-at-74.html?scp=34&sq=obituary+painter&st=nyt

5. Clymer, John Ford. [Obituary] http://www.nytimes .com /1989/ 11/04/ obituaries/john-ford-clymer-painter-82.html ?scp=1&sq=john+ford+clymer&st=nyt

6. Conti, Primo. [Obituary] http://www.nytimes. com/1988/11/13/obituaries/primo-conti-painter-88.html ?scp=1&sq=Primo+Conti+&st=nyt

7. Cotter, Holland. "A mind where Picasso meets Looney Tunes" *The New York Times*, January 27, 2011.

8. Dawkins, Richard. *The selfish gene.* Oxford University Press, 1989.

9. Evans, Minnie. [Obituary] http://www.nytimes .com/1987/12/19/obituaries/minnie-evans-95-folk-painter-noted-for-visionary-work.html?scp=18 &sq=painter +obituary&st=nyt

10. Fischer, Paul M., Meyer P. Schwartz, John W. Richards, Jr., Adam O. Goldstein and Tina H. Rojas. "Brand logo recognition by children aged 3 to 6 years". *Journal of the American Medical Association*, 266, December 11, 1991: 3145-3148.

11. Goffman, Erving. *The presentation of self in everyday life.* Doubleday, 1959

12. "Grant Wood" http://www.artic.edu/ artaccess/AA_Modern/pages/MOD_5.shtml

13. Hayter, Stanley William. [Obituary] http://www.nytimes.com/1988/05/06/obituaries/stanley-

william-hayter-86-dies-painter-taught-miro-and-
pollack.html?scp=3&sq=Stanley+William+Hayter&st=nyt

14. Hogan, Patrick. [Obituary] http://www.nytimes
.com/1988/05/09/obituaries/patrick-hogan-artist-in-california-
is-dead.html?scp=3&sq=Patrick+Hogan&st=nyt

15. Humphrey, Ralph. [Obituary] http://www.nytimes
.com/1990/07/17/obituaries/ralph-humphrey-an-abstract-
painter-and-a-teacher-58.html?scp=5& sq=obituary+
painter&st=nyt

16. Lucie-Smith, Edward. *Art today.* Phaidon, 1999.

17. MacCarthy, Fiona. *Stanley Spencer: An English
vision.* Yale University press, 1997.

18. Phillips, Ann Cole. [Obituary] http://www.nytimes
. com/1990/12/16/obituaries/ann-cole-phillips-84-semi-
abstract-painter.html?scp=11&sq=obituary+painter&st=nyt

19. Pieck, Anton. [Obituary] http://www.nytimes.
com/1987/11/28/obituaries/anton-pieck-painter-92.html?
scp=1&sq=painter+obituary&st=nyt

20. Reinhardt, Ad. *Art-as-art: The selected writings of
Ad Reinhardt,* edited and with an introduction by Barbara
Rose. University of California Press, 1975

21. Searle, John R. *Making the social world: the
structure of human civilization.* Oxford University Press,
2010.

22. Sheets, Millard. [Obituary] http://www.nytimes
.com /1989/04/04/obituaries/millard-sheets-is-dead-arts-
professor-was-81.html?scp=16&sq=obituary+painter&st=nyt

23. Soyer, Raphael. [Obituary] http://www.nytimes.
com/1987/11/05/obituaries/raphael-soyer-social-realist-artist-
is-dead-at-87.html?scp=23&sq=painter+obituary&st=nyt

24. Stahl, Ben. [Obituary] http://www.nytimes.
com/1987/10/24/obituaries/ben-stahl-illustrator-is-dead-a-

founder-of-artists-school.html? scp=13&sq=painter
+obituary&st=nyt

25. Stussy, Jan. [Obituary] http://www.nytimes.
com/1990/08/02/obituaries/jan-stussy-artist-68.html?
scp=51&sq=obituary+painter&st=nyt

26. Tamayo, Rufino. [Obituary] http://www.nytimes.
com/1991/06/25/obituaries/rufino-tamayo-a-leader-in-mexican-
art-dies-at-91.html?scp=38&sq=obituary+painter&st=nyt

27. Thirlwell, Angela. *Into the frame: the four loves of Ford Madox Brown.* Chatto & Windus, 2010.

28. Treuherz, Julian. "Alma-Tadema, aesthete, architect and interior designer" in *Sir Lawrence Alma-Tadema*, edited by Edwin Becker. Rizzoli International Publications, 1997

29. Wagstaff, Marguerite. [Obituary] http://www.
nytimes .com/1990/10/17/obituaries/marguerite-wagstaff-
painter-is-dead-at-91.html? scp=2&sq=obituary
+painter&st=nyt

30. Williams, Neil. [Obituary] http://www.nytimes.
com/1988/03/30/obituaries/neil-williams-painter-on-shaped-
canva s-53.html?scp=2&sq=%22Neil+Williams%22&st=nyt

Paintings live and die

1. Brown, David Alan. *Leonardo's Last Supper: The Restoration.* National Gallery of Art, 1983.

2. Hyde, Lewis. *The Gift: Creativity and the artist in the modern world.* Vintage Books, 2007.

Did I ever paint fifty boat pictures?

1. Stuckey, Charles F. *Claude Monet 1840 - 1926.* The Art Institute of Chicago, 1995.

About the author

Terrence A. Brooks attended three art schools: Shepy International School of Art (Edmonton, Alberta), Vancouver School of Art (Vancouver, BC) and the Nova Scotia School of Art and Design (Halifax, NS). He maintains a personal art website at http://terrybrooksart.com/ He has been a painter for more than fifty years and believes that you should do art every day.

He has been a university professor teaching information technology for thirty years. The two major interests of his life touch when he does web design.